BISHOP MARTIN MARTY:

"THE BLACK ROBE LEAN CHIEF"

by

ROBERT F. KAROLEVITZ

Library of Congress Catalogue No. 80-67366

Privately printed
in the United States of America
for
the Benedictine Sisters of
Sacred Heart Convent
Yankton, South Dakota
57078

Dedicated to the
Sisters of Sacred Heart Convent
and especially to my
teachers:

Sister Genevieve Kaiser
Sister Alphonsa Linster
Sister Rose Marie Bierschbach
Sister Gemma Kranz
Sister Natalie Horacek
and
Sister Martina Dreis

A Foreword

This is the story of an unusual man: a true pioneer of territorial Dakota, a zealous missionary, a humble servant of God and a rather uncomplicated personality whose nature, in contradiction, somehow led him into complex and frustrating confrontations which burdened and undoubtedly shortened his otherwise productive life.

One of the problems inherent in the writing and interpretation of history is that readers too often judge actions and events of the past on the knowledge and biases of a later era. This will very likely be true when some individuals view, in retrospect, the life's work of Bishop Martin Marty, especially his missionary involvement with the Sioux Indians.

Hindsight, they say, is 20/20 vision, so it would be easy to argue, more than a century later, that Bishop Marty might have been wrong in his desire to "civilize" the Indians, cut their hair, turn them into farmers and housewives, and amalgamate the former tribal members into America's socio-economic mainstream as quickly as possible.

Unfortunately, the Bishop and other dedicated missionaries of his day—both Catholic and Protestant—did not have the advantage of the accumulated experience, good and bad, on which detractors of a later generation can pass their after-the-fact judgments. If Bishop Marty was wrong, so too were Presidents of the United States, Congress, representatives of other religious bodies and almost everyone else who attempted to grapple with the immense sociological problem of the era.

As the bits and pieces of Martin Marty's career were being assembled, it quickly became evident that numerous contradictions and inaccuracies have appeared in earlier material written about him. To a degree that was understandable, because his was the kind of life of which legends are made; and although discrepancies cloud the research, none of the points of contention or fictionalized embellishment seem to be significant enough to affect the tone or direction of the overall story in final analysis.

As a youngster during the "Dirty Thirties," I was an acolyte for the late Father Ignatius Forster, O.S.B., who for 27 years was chaplain to the Sisters of Sacred Heart Convent at Yankton, South Dakota. He lived in Bishop Marty's first episcopal residence where we vested for Mass in the adjoining chapel and later were treated in the dining room to a filling breakfast, which was especially welcome during those days of the Great Depression.

There was an aura of the past about the old house, and Father Ignatius was a devoted student of the life of Martin Marty. When I proposed to write a high school theme about the Bishop, he became so interested in the project that I had to be mildly adamant or he would have ghost-written the entire class paper for me. From that experience I retained a somewhat latent desire to pursue a full-scale life story of "The Lean Chief," as the Indians called the pioneer missionary.

Somehow that work kept getting pushed aside, but finally—with the impetus of the Century of Service jubilee of the Sisters of Sacred Heart Convent—I was given the added incentive necessary to complete the much delayed "labor of love." In it I have endeavored to portray Bishop Marty as he really was; to humanize him, not so much to bring him down from the lofty pedestal upon which he's been vaguely remembered through the years, but to present him as the deserving subject of historical biography that he really was.

This, then, is my own special *ora et labora!*

—Robert F. Karolevitz

Chapter I

A Swiss Beginning, An American Challenge

"Here am I; send me!"
—Isaiah, 6:8

In the summer of 1876, the smoldering cauldron of white-Indian animosities in Dakota, Montana and Wyoming Territories erupted into the bloodiest kind of warfare. On the 25th of June that year, Lt. Col. George Armstrong Custer bungled his way into a military disaster on the banks of the Little Big Horn River which not only cost him his own life but sacrificed on the altar of vanity more than 200 troopers of the Seventh Cavalry Regiment.

When survivors were brought out of the battleground on the steamer *Far West* and news of the massacre was tap-tapped to an incredulous world on the telegraph wire from Bismarck, a wave of bitter sentiment against the victorious Sioux and Cheyenne warriors spread across the land. The clamor for retribution was intense and unrelenting as journalists in the East (who may never have seen a redman) colored the story with lurid descriptions of the "scalp-waving savages" desecrating what they labeled the cream of America's soldierhood.

Just two weeks after the debacle on the Little Big Horn, a 42-year-old Benedictine abbot at St. Meinrad monastery in southwestern Indiana made final plans to leave the security of the abbey and travel to the Standing Rock Indian reservation astride the Grand River in the heart of the Dakota Territory.

Abbot Martin Marty, the Swiss-born priest, was filled, not with the prevailing spirit of vengeance but a zealous eagerness to begin his missionary work. He may, in fact have been a little naive about conditions as they actually existed on the prairies, not to mention his limited knowledge of the Indians themselves. White settlement beyond the eastern fringes of what were to become the states of North and South Dakota was slow and spotty. Three years earlier—in 1873—the Northern Pacific Railroad had reached Bismarck, while the Dakota Southern had edged westward along the Missouri River from Sioux City to the territorial capital at Yankton; but, despite this, the tide of immigration had not yet come.

While Abbot Marty was arranging for Prior Fintan Mundwiler to manage the affairs at St. Meinrad in his absence, the interest in Dakota was focused mostly on gold. Thousands of argonauts flocked to the Black Hills in the summer of 1876, flaunting their government's treaty with the Indians. The promise of great wealth to be found in Deadwood Gulch had, in their minds, higher priority than a paper scratched with the signatory X's of illiterate tribesmen.

The majority of non-Indians on the frontier at that time were still primarily opportunists, not farmers. They were, for the most part, exuberant young men in their teens, twenties and early thirties, eager to get in on the ground floor of settlement, government position and the lucrative business of supply to Indian agencies and military outposts. The discovery of gold came as an obvious bonus opportunity.

So the mood of the whites (other than the religious missionaries of various denominations already on the scene) was

Martin Marty was just 26 years old when he first came to the U. S. He was 37 when he became the abbot of St. Meinrad Abbey. (St. Meinrad Archabbey archives)

more for subjugation and even eradication of the Indians rather than for Christianization or civilization. And after the massacre at Little Big Horn, that feeling was intensified among the civilians and kept seething in the ranks of military men awaiting a proper moment for vengeance.

Abbot Martin may have known or suspected some of this, but it was far overshadowed by his unquestioning desire to begin the labors he felt destined to pursue even before he left the Benedictine monastery of Maria Einsiedeln in Switzerland sixteen years earlier. In his own words, he revealed his personal motivation dating back to the days of his novitiate: "... divine grace gave me the urge to do what nobody else wanted to do ... I have always been guided by this rule and perhaps also specially blessed therein."

His opportunity came when the struggling two-year-old Bureau of Catholic Indian Missions was frustrated in its attempts to find someone to take over the missionary responsibilities at the Standing Rock Reservation in its remote, uninviting location. Father J. B. A. Brouillet, director-general of the bureau (known in the beginning as the Office of the Catholic Commissioner for Indian Missions), learning of Marty's interest in the Sioux, exchanged correspondence with him in the spring of 1876. The result was an offer from the abbot to send two priests to Dakota temporarily to take care of the untended spiritual needs of the moment and to determine what sort of arrangement might be made to serve the region permanently.

It is tradition at St. Meinrad that when Abbot Marty spoke to the assembled monks and asked for volunteers, the first to respond was 46-year-old Father Chrysostom Foffa, who had been one of the earliest priests to come to Indiana from Einsiedeln in 1855. A giant of a man by physical standards of the day, he was six feet, two inches tall and weighed some 220 pounds, combining with his size a boyish enthusiasm which he still retained after more than 20 years of struggle to bring permanence and stability to the monastery at St. Meinrad.

After Father Chrysostom had made his commitment, the abbot paused momentarily and then said: "You are the one, and I am the second."

The slightly built Father Marty—four inches shorter and more than 80 pounds lighter than his missionary partner—then included 20-year-old Brother Giles Laugel as the third member of the pioneering group. The stage was accordingly set for the abbot to begin what Prior Fintan later wrote was "a more grateful field of work among the Indians than here [in Indiana] among the Germans."

To understand the situation into which Abbot Marty was injecting himself and possibly the resources of St. Meinrad as well, it is necessary to reflect upon the policy of the United States government relative to missionary activities among the Indians at that time.

In 1869 Ulysses Simpson Grant, hero of the Civil War, came into the presidency without political experience to head a nation beset with the unresolved problems of reconstruction and a host of other nagging domestic difficulties. Among the latter was the graft-ridden management of the Indian reservations. Under the prevailing system, agents—who got their assignments largely as the result of political payoff—grew rich on the $1,500-a-year jobs. Corruption was rampant; and the Indians, who were supposed to be the beneficiaries of the program, became the victims instead.

In his inaugural address, President Grant revealed his support of any course which would lead the Indians "to civilization and citizenship." With the urging of various religious pressure groups, led principally by the Quakers, Congress responded with what became known as the Grant Peace Policy, enacted on April 10, 1869. Under the law, Christian organizations, acting in harmony with the federal government, were to take over the management, education and physical well-being of reservation-bound tribes, as well as their evangelization. As the policy developed, specific denominations were assigned exclusively to the various reservations, and agents were appointed by the respective church bodies to assure the impartation of "good Christian principles" and the end to profiteering and thievery.

Theoretically high-principled as it may have seemed at the time, the "peace policy" did not account for inter-denominational rivalries which created a whole new set of problems. In Dakota Territory, reservations were parcelled out to three groups: Episcopalians, Catholics and the American Board of Commissioners for Foreign Missions, a joint Congregational and Presbyterian organization. The Episcopalians, because of their greater political influence at the time, got the lion's share. Catholic control was assigned to Devils Lake and Standing Rock agencies, and it was to minister to the latter that Abbot Martin of St. Meinrad had received his call.

Catholic action following implementation of the "peace policy" had been woefully laggard. Lack of an organized effort at both the national and territorial levels had permitted six years to elapse without substantive activities on the reservations. Indians who had been instructed and baptized by earlier itinerant missionary priests—notably Father Pierre Jean De Smet, Father Christian Hoecken and Father Augustin Ravoux—retained only vague impressions of the faith after many intervening years without visitations by the "black robes." What's more, noting Catholic inactivity, the Protestant churches were casting acquisitive eyes on the poorly served agencies.

Marty was concerned about the failure of his Church to assume a greater responsibility among the Indians. Though his Dakota sojourn was supposed to be temporary, before he left St. Meinrad, he had his choir stall removed and ordered Prior Fintan to take over the room he had occupied as head of the monastery. This was, of course, a rather obvious hint that the abbot was thinking in terms of an extended absence rather than a short one.

On July 11 he boarded the train for Dakota, leaving Father Chrysostom and Brother Giles behind in Indiana until he could make a preliminary assessment of conditions and needs. Eight days later the Dakota Southern chugged into Yankton, the territorial capital, and Abbot Martin stepped down expectantly onto

The missionary work of Father Pierre Jean De Smet had an early influence on young Martin Marty who read about the peripatetic Jesuit during his studies at Einsiedeln. (South Dakota State Historical Society)

the railroad platform which was, in effect, the threshold to his new career.

What lay ahead, he undoubtedly wondered? Would he be able to realize his dream of imparting Benedictine ideals to a nomadically inclined people whose language he couldn't speak? Would *ora et labora*—pray and work—prevail as effectively on the Dakota plains as it had for more than twelve centuries in Europe?

Eagerly he sought out Father Valentine Sommereisen, the resident priest in Yankton, so that he might find a place to say Mass. As legend has it, he was not prepared at all for the inhospitable greeting he was to receive. Father Sommereisen, an irascible and suspicious German priest at odds with his predominantly Irish congregation, denied the abbot the use of the chapel for his priestly offering because Marty failed to produce a *celebret,* the customary letter from his bishop or superior signifying that the bearer was free from canonical censure.

It was not the first obstacle Father Martin Marty had faced in the pursuit of his service to God, and assuredly it would not be the last. Stung by the rebuff but undeterred in his mission, he then made arrangements for steamboat passage up the Missouri to Standing Rock, confident that now, as in the past, he would receive sufficient grace to help him "do what nobody else wanted to do."

✠ ✠ ✠

The long road from the Swiss mountainside to the flatlands of Dakota began for Martin Marty on January 12, 1834. He was the

Yankton, Dakota Territory, in the mid-1870s was a typical frontier village when Abbot Martin first arrived at the territorial capital. In a few short years it was to become his episcopal see city. (Yankton County Historical Society)

first of eleven children born to a shoemaker and church sexton, James Joseph Alois Marty, and his wife, Elizabeth Reichlin, a former servant girl, in the small Alpine city of Schwyz. Within 24 hours of his birth (according to custom), the infant was taken to St. Martin's Church where he was christened Joseph Melchoir Alois, the name he was to bear for the first 21 years of his life.

Schwyz, in the predominantly Catholic canton of the same name, lies in the uncommonly beautiful valley between the Lake of Lucerne (the Vierwaldstätter See) and Lake Zurich. The jagged crags of the Mythen peaks rise above the diminutive orchards and farm fields confined to the inter-mountain vale. In this picturesque Christmas-card setting, Sexton Marty—as the Schwyzers called

Schwyz, in the Swiss canton of the same name, was the birthplace of the future Dakota bishop. (Sacred Heart Convent library)

him—worked diligently at his cobbler's bench to support a growing family, raised under the comforting, unquestioned mantle of traditional Catholicism.

When Alois was not yet two, however, that faith was severely put to test. As the young boy played beside his father, he was inquisitively drawn to the tempting tools and trappings which lay within easy reach of tiny fingers. On the bench was a bottle of acid mixed with tallow, used by shoemakers of the day to treat and polish the leather they were working. Parents of all generations know the lightning-like speed with which childish hands can reach out for dangerous substances, and it was in such a frightening instant that Alois grabbed the bottle and began to drink its contents.

Undoubtedly the bitter taste of the vitriol dissuaded the youngster from swallowing the toxic potion, but the acid was so caustic that it left lifelong scars where it ran down his chin and onto his unprotected feet. Panic-stricken, the child's parents—still in their twenties—turned emotionally to the one remedy which occurred to them in their distress. They prayed!

The painful burns inside the child's mouth and on his tongue were so severe that the swelling threatened to choke him. "Spare him," the mother and father appealed, as they tearfully promised a pilgrimage to the shrine of Maria-Sonnenberg if the Blessed Virgin would intercede for their son's recovery. An apparently miraculous cure resulted, and the future bishop suffered no impairment of speech nor damage to the rich voice which he himself would lift in songs of thanksgiving throughout his lifetime at the altars of two continents. (An *ex voto* tablet placed by the grateful shoemaker and his wife on Mount Seelis in the neighboring canton of Uri has attested to the fulfillment of their vow.)

Never a robust child, Alois was nonetheless active and precocious. At the age of five he began attending the Jesuit preparatory school at Kloesterli. At a time when it was customary

Martin Marty was born in a room above the ground-floor shoemaker's shop in this building in Schwyz. Pictured are Leodegar Stutz, Marty's brother-in-law; Father Martin Marty, who confusingly shared his older brother's monastic name; the bishop's mother and sister. (Sacred Heart Convent archives)

to withold the Eucharist from children until they were twelve years old, he received his First Communion there on April 30, 1843, when he was only nine. That same year he finished his primary schooling and was ready to enter the Gymnasium or "middle school" which was also conducted by the Jesuits in Schwyz.

Though he was one of the youngest members of his class, Marty excelled, not only in his studies, but in music as well. Meanwhile, it was not unusual for him to be at St. Martin's Church at five in the morning, help his father in the sacristy, serve at several consecutive Masses and then hurry to school—often without breakfast—to be in time for the students' Mass there. So dedicated was he that the Jesuit teachers asked his father to send the boy to the Gymnasium of their St. Michael's College at Fribourg, southwest of Bern, where he might add to his list of studies the French language for which he showed a proficiency.

To ease the financial burden on Sexton Marty, the Jesuits offered Alois a scholarship based on his musical ability. His services as an organist and singer would offset his board and tuition costs, they said. Realistically, they were making an investment in him as a promising vocation for the Society of Jesus. As a result, in the fall of 1846 he went to St. Michael's College to begin his fourth year of secondary schooling.

The academic atmosphere at Fribourg was intellectually stimulating to the talented, striving young Schwyzer; and a career as a Jesuit priest appealed to him. There were, however, serious rumblings of political dissension within Switzerland which, as it turned out, were to have a major effect on Alois Marty's future.

In the 1830s a strong move for a liberal revision of the Swiss constitution had begun. As a counter development, the Catholic cantons of Lucerne, Uri, Schwyz, Unterwalden, Fribourg and Valais created a separatist confederation called the Sonderbund. In May of 1847 a majority of the 22 cantons voted to dissolve what was considered to be an illegal union. The minority, however—in the name of religion and states rights—was determined to resist by force.

Unfortunately for the separatists, the Protestant cantons had superior troops, equipment and economic advantage; and the Sonderbund War—as it was called—proved to be short-lived. Thirteen-year-old Alois Marty left Fribourg which capitulated on November 14, 1847. Zug surrendered a week later, and on November 23, the final battles were fought at Meierskappel and Gislikon. From a vantage point on the Uetliberg, Marty was able to see the smoke of cannons and to hear the sounds of gunfire at the latter site.

With the defeat of the outmanned Sonderbund forces, Lucerne was occupied, while nuns and Jesuit priests fled by steamer to

Martin Marty's father was sexton in the parish church at Schwyz in addition to his work as a shoemaker. His oldest son served Mass and assisted him in the sacristy as he was introduced to religious responsibilities at an early age. (Sacred Heart Convent archives)

Flüelen and then over the St. Gotthard Pass to exile. Confused as he was by the turn of events, Alois returned home to Schwyz to await developments. In 1848 a new federal state was proclaimed with a revised constitution which guaranteed freedom of the press, worship, association and settlement. However, by a strangely narrow interpretation, religious liberty did not include the Jesuits who were forced to abandon their schools and leave the country.

Though the Catholic cantons lost the war and their fight against the liberalized constitution, religious convictions and practices were not disrupted nor limited except where the Society of Jesus was concerned. Somehow the educational gap created by their expulsion had to be filled, and the Benedictine monasteries responded. On December 21, less than a month after he had witnessed the battle at Gislikon, Alois Marty was enrolled at the nine-centuries-old Abbey of Our Lady of Einsiedeln in his home canton of Schwyz.

Einsiedeln—from the German word for "hermitage"—dates back to approximately 828 A.D. when St. Meinrad, a Benedictine monk, received permission to serve God as a hermit, settling in the forest at the foot of Mount Etzel about two miles from Lake Zurich, a secluded spot he had discovered during a fishing trip. He lived there for seven years, but when so many visitors began to disturb his saintly solitude, he moved some three and a half miles deeper into what was known as the Dark Forest.

Here, beside his simple hut, he built a small chapel dedicated to the Blessed Virgin Mary. For 26 more years he worked and prayed in seclusion, although pious penitents continued to make pilgrimages to his shrine.

In 861 two men appeared at the chapel just as the monk was concluding his thanksgiving after Mass. It soon became evident that their intention was to rob the hermit of whatever valuables he might have received from pilgrims grateful for his counsel. After searching the shrine and finding nothing, they turned on St. Meinrad whom they had seen hiding something inside his habit. Angrily, they beat the holy man until he was dead, discovering afterwards that the only treasure he had attempted to save were small relics from the altar.

Tradition has it that the murderers were followed by the monk's two pet ravens which screeched in angry retribution

The town of Einsiedeln is located in the Sihl Lake valley in central Switzerland northeast of Schwyz. Its name comes from the German word for "hermitage," and dates back approximately to 828 A.D. when St. Meinrad led a life of prayerful seclusion nearby. (Sacred Heart Convent archives)

as the villains hurried away from the scene of their crime. When the men reached the nearest village, the people recognized the birds and suspecting that something was wrong, they arrested the two strangers. Later, when St. Meinrad's body was found, the robbers were burned at the stake.

Thereafter, the shrine attracted an increasing number of pilgrimages, and in 934 St. Eberhard established a monastery on the site known as St. Meinrad's Cell. In 1073 it became Einsiedeln which, in turn, had its periods of prosperity and adversity through the years.

Education at the monastery had been confined for almost eight centuries almost exclusively to the needs of the Benedictines themselves. With the change of conditions in Switzerland, though, it became apparent that Catholic schooling beyond the primary level would be seriously affected by the departure of the Jesuits. That was why at Einsiedeln a new curriculum was developed to accommodate more young men who may or may not ultimately be attracted to the monastic life.

Starting belatedly in the semester as he did, Alois Marty had to adjust to the new surroundings and teaching methods, but despite that, he still earned top honors in the fifth-year Gymnasium class in history and French. His academic capabilities were quickly recognized, even by his fellow students, as the following verses translated from the student publication, the *Wahrheitsfreund,* described him:

> Hey, look here, what childlike features!
> Yet one of those roguish creatures;
> Though he's lived but fourteen years,
> He's got stuff behind his ears.
>
> Now I hear his voice resounding,
> Through the woods its echoes bounding.
> Truly, here's a real boy;
> Even studies are his joy.

The present Benedictine monastery of Maria Einsiedeln, where Martin Marty was educated and ordained, was built between 1704 and 1735 and reputedly is one of the finest examples of Baroque architecture in Switzerland. (Verkehrsverein Einsiedeln)

The shoemaker's son from Schwyz continued to excel as he completed his sixth and final class in the Gymnasium and prepared to enter the two-year Lyceum course. In addition to his studies, he sang in the choir and played in the orchestra and band. Besides the piano and organ, he apparently had some ability with the violin, bass horn and bombardon, a bassoon-type instrument. To help pay his way (his parents by this time had seven other living children), he tutored foreign students in the German language, and received an honorarium for translating the French *Annals of the Propagation of the Faith* into German.

The visit of Bishop John Henni to Einsiedeln in 1848 helped spur Martin Marty's interest in America. Almost 40 years later he was to write Henni's biography. (Sacred Heart Convent library)

It was during his work with the *Annals* that he became acquainted with the experiences of Father Pierre Jean De Smet, the peripatetic Jesuit missionary, who was then ministering to the Indians in a far-away place called Dakota. Earlier, in the summer of 1848, a visitor from the New World—Bishop John Martin Henni of Milwaukee, Wisconsin—had been entertained by the students at Einsiedeln as he sought priests for his many German parishioners. Though Alois Marty did not immediately give evidence of an interest in America, there is little doubt but that a slowly germinating seed had been planted.

Chapter II

A Mountainside Ordeal, A Monastic Call

"I will watch my ways, so as not to sin with my tongue; I will set a curb on my mouth."

—Psalms, 39:2

On June 15, 1852, Father Joseph Kundek, vicar general of the diocese of Vincennes, Indiana, arrived at Einsiedeln on a recruiting mission. He and his bishop—Maurice de St. Palais—were touring Europe, looking for German-speaking priests to fill a growing need in America and especially in south central Indiana where the dynamic Croatian priest had been actively promoting German immigration. As the result of his work, the towns of Ferdinand and Celestine had been established in Dubois County; and, with very little help, he had been serving the Catholic families which settled along the north-south road from Jasper to the Ohio River port of Troy, where Abraham Lincoln and his father once operated a ferry.

As it turned out, Father Kundek's visit couldn't have been more strategically timed!

After the Sonderbund War, which had seriously depleted the resources of the various Swiss monasteries, the religious unrest had continued. Furthermore, in the canton of Ticino, the government had forced the monks from Einsiedeln out of the college at Bellinzona which they had operated since 1675. This occurred less than three weeks before the priest from Indiana arrived; and the mood of Abbot Henry IV Schmid von Baar and his fellow Benedictines was susceptible to overtures of a potential place of refuge in America if conditions continued to worsen.

With the release of the faculty at Bellinzona, Abbot Henry had the personnel for a substantial venture; but his decision, approved by Rome, was to move cautiously and to send just two priests to America to see if the establishment of a foundation or daughter-house might be feasible. For the task he chose Father Ulrich Christen, a serious-minded, highly-opinionated Swiss native, and Father Bede O'Connor, London-born son of poor Irish parents who, as a youngster of 14, had been taken to Einsiedeln where he learned to speak and write German as perfectly as his native English.

On the day before their scheduled departure for the United States on December 19, 1852, a farewell program was planned, and 18-year-old Alois Marty was put in charge of the student entertainment, consisting of speeches, poetry recitations and musical selections. In the final oration which he himself delivered, Marty compared the activities of sixth and nineteenth century Benedictines.

He likened the sending of priests to the New World to an earlier dispersal of Black Monks (as the Benedictines were known) into the pagan areas of Europe where they established the great centers of Christian culture and paved the way for the glories of the Middle Ages. Prophetically, he referred to America in his prologue as "the land of the future," and hailed the action of Einsiedeln in undertaking a Benedictine foundation there. "Today," he said, "we are celebrating the birthday of an event which in due time and for a series of centuries is . . . to be rich in achievements and blessings."

Abbot Henry IV Schmid von Baar of the Benedictine monastery of Maria Einsiedeln played a key role in Martin Marty's life. It was he who sent the young priest to America on the "temporary" assignment which lasted for 36 years. (Maria Einsiedeln archives)

Viewed in retrospect, young Marty—whether knowingly or unknowingly—may have been setting the stage for his own career, a missionary commitment which he referred to as the return of the Benedictine Order to its "original historical destiny."

As a student of the Lyceum, Alois Marty studied English in addition to his other subjects. In extra-curricular activities he was first editor of the *Zeitgeist*, a weekly publication of cartoons and commentary about the school and its students. With ready wit and an excess of energy, he was a natural leader. His weakness, a tendency toward sarcasm and biting retort, grew out of his mental quickness and impatience with others who were slower to respond. Giving early evidence of a life-long devotion to the Mother of God, he took the lead in establishing the Sodality of the Blessed Virgin Mary among the students at Einsiedeln, having become acquainted with the organization during his stay at Fribourg.

Yet, as seemingly successful as he was in his school pursuits, Alois suffered a blow to his pride when the monastery superiors rejected his application to the novitiate until he could bring his self-assertive nature under control. However, instead of discouraging him or making him resentful, the rebuff spurred him to greater effort to prove his fitness to wear the Benedictine habit. At that critical point in his life, a tragic event occurred which was to help him immeasurably in the transition from exuberant youth to responsible manhood.

On September 29, 1853, his sister Elizabeth, one year younger than he, fell victim to typhoid fever. Her death was a crushing blow to Alois, who—in the jargon of a later generation—was at the time desperately "trying to find himself." Home for the autumnal vacation which lasted from August 16 to October 28, he was torn by grief and personal frustration. The depths of his feelings can best be expressed in excerpts from his own words written after the sad occasion:

> ". . . All human society, life itself, was loathsome to me. During the mornings I remained in my room and prayed the Office of the Dead for my sister. In the afternoons I left the house as quickly as possible, not to enter it again until late in the evening. On those occasions I sought the most lonely roads and places where I could hope that no one would meet me.
>
> "Either I directed my steps to one of the surrounding mountains . . . or I took along Hammer's *Lehrbuch der Geschichte* . . . to a quiet, untrodden spot I had discovered at the foot of the Haggen. I sat under one of the trees alongside the rippling brook and read . . . or with my eyes followed the course of the brook which reminded me of my own destiny."

He then wrote of the consoling thought of eventually joining his sister in heaven and of the depressing burden of the trials which would undoubtedly face him before he, too, reached the goal. He chided himself unmercifully for the brusqueness and aloofness with which he had too often responded to her love.

> "I remembered all the joys she had prepared for me, all the love she had given me so undeserved; and with sorrow I thought how badly I had, with hardness and unkindness, requited her for all that. Only now had I become aware that to her I had been the dearest thing in the world.
>
> "Then I took my recourse to God . . . and with sundown prayed my rosary, offering it for the repose of her dear soul. It afforded me consolation to be able to show her my love at least in this manner."

For two weeks he continued his sad estrangement from the world and the personal reproachment which accompanied his actions. On October 13—the fourteenth day after Elizabeth's death—he again left the house:

> "My father, whether it was a premonition or whether my manner of life pained him, begged me not to go too far away and to come home again by three o'clock. I answered that the weather was fair, and I did not know where I was going nor when I was coming home . . .
>
> "I sauntered off, and finally, to forget all else by hiking, I resolved to carry out a long-harbored plan to climb the highest peak of the Urmi Mountains which lay before me. I went down along Lake Lowerz and, having passed that, began gradually to go up toward the mountain . . . it was one o'clock in the afternoon . . . I felt I ought to go home, but I did not . . .
>
> "A man who had his left hand wound about with a white cloth came up along the same road. We exchanged a few words, and in bidding farewell, I wished him a good recovery; he was the last human being I was to see that day. Now I briskly strode forward up the mountain. I met with but little worth noticing [although] a black cat for a long time ran ahead of me, and, as I turned from the fields and meadows into the forest, the crying and crowing of birds met me from all sides . . .
>
> "It was three o'clock. Meanwhile, I had arrived at the foot of the highest rocky peak . . . that towered upwards perpendicularly in front of me. I found no way of climbing it, and in vain I tried repeatedly and from several sides to scale it; the crumbling rubble always forced me back. I finally gave up that plan as impossible and turned toward the western side of the mountain where a deep cut separates it from Rigi-Scheidegg. There I by-passed the peak and for some time delighted myself at the sight of Gersau—where my

second-oldest sister, Magdalena, served as nursemaid—and of the magnificent Vierwaldstätter See . . .

"I now went at random along the mountain till I came to a newly built hut, but I found nobody there. Not far away was a road. From its direction I concluded that it came from Gersau . . . It ran squarely across a spur of the mountain, and I climbed to its crest and from there saw below me still other similar spurs . . . I stood a long time and sang some songs, I no longer know what . . . it was half past four.

"At that time I resolved to hurry home on the shortest route before night. I again looked for my old path and stepped along it lively and in good spirits . . . I finally came to a high ledge that may have been about three or four feet wide and was covered with felled firs. On the outside was a sheer drop into a ravine; above me rock walls stretched upwards."

By then it was five o'clock, and Alois, intent on finding a short-cut, decided to work his way down into the deep ravine, holding onto the tufts of grass growing out of the rocks. (He learned later that had he followed the ascending trail a bit farther, he would have come to some houses and an easy descent, but he chose otherwise in his desire to spare his parents the worry of his tardiness.)

He threw his hat and walking stick down into the ravine ahead of him, using both hands to keep himself from falling into the deep gorge, at the end of which he hoped to find a road or footpath. When he reached the bottom, however, he found another sheer drop down to the lake, and by this time it was beginning to grow dark. He couldn't go back the way he had come, so—with a fervent prayer—he again started downward, trusting that fir seedlings and the clumps of grass he clutched would not break loose and send him tumbling down into the abyss.

Almost miraculously he accomplished the descent, finally reaching an almost dry stream bed which he felt certain would lead him down to the lake. He began to quicken his pace as he grew confident of a safe delivery.

Meanwhile, back in Schwyz the Marty family was deeply concerned about his late return. They also prayed, and for the second time in their son's life, his parents vowed to make a pilgrimage to the shrine of Our Lady on Maria-Sonnenberg. They would go annually, they entreated, if he would be brought safely home. Alois, however, was undergoing a harrowing, painful ordeal whose outcome was considerably in doubt.

"How the fall happened, I do not know. The first thing I recall is

. . . I heard someone whimpering. After long listening . . . I became aware that it was from myself. Is it you? Do these limbs that burn so and this beaten head belong to you? Is that blood trickling down on your forehead? Impossible! A thing like this cannot happen to you . . .

"Where am I lying? How did I get here? Feel yourself. But I cannot move a limb! It is only a dream!

"Gradually I . . . dimly recalled the happenings of the past few hours, opened my eyes, saw the moon rising between the clouds, felt the raw night air; and now my situation dawned on me with terrible clearness . . . I slowly regained the use of my limbs. When I stretched out my hand, I reached into ice-cold water that only now I heard rushing by, and . . . I became aware that I was lying in the bed of a brook.

"After long and unsuccessful exertions, I succeeded in . . . reaching the bank, about two steps distant; there, half leaning, half lying, with a foot braced against a stone, I sought some rest. With little change, that remained my position till morning.

"Before that I had tried without success to quench my thirst with water from the brook. My left hand was enlarged and bled from a deep, open wound; my left eye was all beaten up and swollen. From my forehead blood constantly flowed down over my face; my teeth were quite loose and pieces of them filled my mouth; my whole body was bruised and torn . . .

"I gradually began to think: my condition, my future, my death, my past, my dear ones at home and elsewhere—all that filled me with unspeakable pain. All the stories of rescues that had been told me passed through my phantasy; yet none would apply to me. I made an attempt to call out, but I could not . . .

"Now I recalled that I had not yet prayed my rosary that day and began to make up for the omission; I no longer know how far I got with that . . . I again lost consciousness . . . It may have been one o'clock when I noticed a rather strong rain which lasted intermittently till six o'clock in the morning. The chill of the night air had become penetrating, whereas the rain cooled my burning limbs and, as I opened my mouth, partly eased my thirst; only I had to fear that the wetness of the ground would make my descent considerably more difficult . . . With some effort I took out my watch and found that the glass had been shattered to dust-like bits . . .

"The question now was: what to do? If I remained lying there, I would constantly be losing strength. No human being could be in the neighborhood; nobody would pass by; hence, either perish in that place or go forward. With unspeakable difficulty and pain, I finally succeeded in raising myself. I first washed the blood from my left eye . . . I could use it for a few minutes, but soon it was again pasted shut with running blood . . . I thought I saw my hat a few steps away from me, but when I came to it, it was a stone.

"Hereupon, guided by Divine Providence, I turned left; had I turned right, as on the previous day, I should most certainly have fallen into a deep crevasse where nobody would ever have found me. Between trees and brush I now crawled diagonally down the mountain till I reached a jutting spot from which my halfblinded eye saw the lake and its shore. What a joy I felt at that!

"... Below me, at a distance of about half an hour stood a house toward which I now aimed to go. The steamboat came along the lake, and shortly thereafter another boat. Still, for some time I had to climb down between rocks and high grass, being able to use only my right hand; if the left hit against anything, a pain shot through me that for a few moments lamed my strength and presence of mind ...

"I reached an oak forest and in it a road that led on to a meadow and down through it to the farmhouse I had seen from above. The road was slippery; several times I fell to the ground. About three minutes above the farmhouse stood a barn. From there I saw at a little distance two boys who looked me over with wary eyes. I beckoned them to come to me and seated myself on the threshold of the upper door of the barn to await them. The mother had sent the boys to look me over ... and because I came along all covered with blood and bent over, I appeared to them to be a big black fellow. They took me for a rascal, of whom they were afraid all the more because on the previous day milk had been stolen from them and the father was not at home.

"Upon the report of the boys, the mother resolved to arm herself and the boys with clubs and so go to meet me. They finally decided that they could overpower me without such instruments so they came up without them to the stable where I sat. When they saw me, they indeed felt quite differently. They led me into the house and took care of me as best they could ...

"After a rest of two hours, at eleven o'clock, they put me in their boat and rowed me over to Brunnen; there they put me in a carriage which brought me to Schwyz ... Now I was at the end of my strength. I lay unconscious on my bed for quite a while. I received the holy sacrament of the dying, and, after that was done, the state of unconsciousness returned and lasted with interruptions for three days."

And so the painful episode ended. Later, on investigation, it was discovered that Alois had fallen more than 65 feet over a sheer precipice onto the rocks below. A jagged gash from the top of his forehead to the base of his nose was filled with grit and would leave an evidential scar for the remainder of his life. However, there were no apparent internal injuries, and his badly swollen left eye was not permanently affected.

Oddly enough, the ring finger of his left hand had received the most damage in the fall as the first phalange was driven back into the palm, leaving him with a shortened, inflexible finger. This, of course, was serious enough because of its effect on his musicianship; but even more discouraging to him was the fact that

From the great artistically ornate religious edifices of Europe—such as the parish church in Schwyz—Martin Marty was to travel to the humblest of shacks and Sioux Indian shelters on the Dakota prairies. (Sacred Heart Convent archives)

the physical defect would bar him from the novitiate at Einsiedeln.

Medical science in 1853 was still dominated by folk remedies and ignorant quackery. A local physician, with no better treatment to offer, suggested that Alois soak the injured finger as often as possible in the warm blood of a newly slaughtered animal and then pull on it forcefully until the knuckle cracked. At an abattoir in Schwyz, arrangements were made to try the unusual therapy, and apparently it worked. The finger was restored to its natural length and dexterity, and eagerly young Marty applied again for acceptance at Einsiedeln.

This time the monks were convinced that their talented, persistent student did indeed have a vocation and had curbed his prideful impatience sufficiently to be reconsidered. On May 19, 1854, he was invested with the habit of St. Benedict and became Novice Alois Marty.

Because he was still a minor, however, he required parental consent. His mother, who later was to give three other sons—John, Anton and Martin (not to be confused with his older brother)—to the priesthood, was especially reluctant to "lose" him to the monastic life and possibly to missionary service beyond Switzerland. She preferred that he become a secular priest, maybe some day even to become pastor of St. Martin's Church in Schwyz where, as a boy, he had helped his father toll the Angelus, played the organ and responded many times to the priest at the foot of the Altar: *"Ad deum qui laetificat juventutem meum."* Ultimately the sincerity of his desire convinced his parents that his call to the Benedictine Rule was a God-given summons, and they acquiesced dutifully to his wishes.

✠ ✠ ✠

Meanwhile, there was the promised pilgrimage to the shrine at Maria-Sonnenberg in thanksgiving for the safe return of Alois from his ordeal on the mountain. For as many years as they were able, family members made the annual visitation to Canton Uri, traveling on foot to Brunnen, crossing the Vierwaldstätter See by boat to the Treib, then making the strenuous climb, first to the Seelisberg and on beyond to the Sonnenberg. Enroute the father never failed to point out to the younger Marty children the white wall of rock high up on the Urmi mountain where their older brother miraculously escaped death.

At the shrine they prayed a grateful rosary of fifteen decades;

and as many other pilgrims had done in commemoration of their own special intentions, they placed a second *ex voto* tablet. Its small painting portrayed a youthful figure fallen over a precipice, with Sexton Marty, his wife and six of their children praying ardently as the image of the Blessed Virgin looked down from the cliff-top. The inscription, evidently written by Alois himself, said:

> "Through your all-powerful intercession, O most blessed Virgin Mary, I have on my vow to Sonnenberg, on October 13 to 14, 1853, been saved and have again recovered from deadly wounds and bruises that I received in my frightful fall . . ."

Chapter III

A Benedictine Forever

"Now the tools are in your hands. Your assignment is to fashion, with God's help, the most exquisite work of art—your monastic life."

—The Rule of St. Benedict

At the age of twenty, Novice Marty began his new life at Einsiedeln. Transformed by his sister's death and the harrowing experience on the mountain—not to mention the humbling effect of being rejected in his first attempts to enter the novitiate—Alois gave himself totally to his theological studies and the demands of the Benedictine regimen.

During his year of monastic probation, he arose with his three fellow novices at four a.m., often during the cold winter months breaking the ice in his wash basin before reporting to the choir room for morning prayer. Each day was rigorously scheduled from the rising hour to retirement again at 8:30 p.m., a program requiring stern discipline of body and mind.

When the first half year of the novitiate was completed, Father Claudius Perrot, the novice master who was to become a noted ascetic writer, reported to the assembled monks that Marty was progressing well in all aspects of his temporary commitment (especially in obedience), and that his physical health had improved.

The final six months passed quickly, and the chapter was again informed of Novice Marty's worthiness. Consequently, on May 29, 1855, with Abbot Henry Schmid officiating at the Pontifical High Mass, the shoemaker's son consecrated himself irrevocably to the service of God by professing the vows of poverty, chastity, obedience, stability and conversion of morals according to the Rule of St. Benedict. At the same time Alois Marty became Martin Marty as he accepted his new religious name in honor of the patron saint of Switzerland and his own parish church in Schwyz, St. Martin of Tours.

As impressive as the voicing of his Benedictine vows was to him personally, the occasion was doubly memorable because at the same Mass the doctrine of the Immaculate Conception of the Blessed Virgin was solemnly proclaimed at Einsiedeln. On the previous December 8, 1854, Pope Pius IX—Giovanni Maria Mastai-Ferretti, whose pontificate from 1846 to 1878 was the longest in the history of the Church—had announced to the world that Mary, the mother of Jesus, was without the taint of original sin from the moment of her own conception. Martin Marty, who had good reason to believe that he owed his life twice to the intercession of Mary, cherished the happy coincidence during which Abbot Henry's reading of the dogmatic decree was accompanied by a chorus of bells and cannon salutes which reverberated across the Swiss countryside. His investiture in the Order of St. Benedict couldn't have been more auspicious.

St. Benedict of Nursia, according to the only known authority of facts about his life—Book Two of the Dialogues *of Pope Gregory I—was born with his twin sister,*

St. Benedict of Nursia left a lasting imprint on an everchanging world through the 73 chapters of his noted Rule and establishment of the Benedictine Order. (Sacred Heart Convent archives)

Scholastica, near Spoleto in the Apennine Mountains some 70 miles northeast of Rome. Although the exact year of his birth is conjectural, it was presumably in 480 A.D. Benedict's parents apparently were landowners of sufficient wealth, permitting them to send their son off to school in the Italian capital when the time came. Beyond that, Pope Gregory (who got his information from four elderly monks who had known St. Benedict in his earlier years) recounted little else of the future saint's childhood in the Umbrian hills.

In Rome young Benedict was said to have been appalled by the unfettered lifestyle of fellow students, so much so that he fled the historic city with Cyrilla, his servant-nurse who filled the role of a "second mother." They established themselves in the village of Enfide where the first evidence of Benedict's spiritual powers was revealed. In her attempt to bake bread for them, Cyrilla had borrowed a terra cotta sieve with which to sift the flour. By accident, she had dropped and broken the baked-clay utensil, a happenstance which had upset her severely. Understandably concerned, Benedict picked up the fragments, took them to his room, offered a prayer, and when he looked up, the sieve was whole again. The elderly nurse, in her delight and amazement, spread the word of the miracle throughout the countryside, and soon Benedict was besieged by people anxious to see and benefit from his obvious supernatural gift.

He fled again, this time alone, to a cave in the rocky highlands near Subiaco. At first only a friend named Romanus knew of his whereabouts; and it was Romanus who brought him bread and other supplies which were lowered in a basket with a long rope from a ledge above the cavern. In time goat-tenders and shepherds in the area became acquainted with the young man who possessed a great gift of teaching. Later, people from throughout the region came to hear him preach in his remote hideaway. Among the latter was a delegation of monks whose mission it was to urge Benedict to come to their monastery as their abbot, even though he was not a priest.

At first he refused, but when they persisted so strongly, he finally relented. Abbot Benedict, however, was not the lenient master the monks had expected. They had been without leadership for a considerable period and had grown lax and free-spirited. Soon they began to resent the new abbot's authority. In fact, several monks, of less noble character, were so incensed by his enforcement of monastic obligations that they resolved to kill him. Poison was mixed with wine in his meal-time goblet, but when Benedict raised his hands above the vessel in blessing, it miraculously shattered.

Whether because of that incident or some other circumstance, Benedict left the unfriendly abbey and returned to the cave where he had already spent three years of his life. Again, hundreds of visitors came to see and hear him. Then it was that he entered into a new role. As his followers increased, he sent groups of them out to establish monasteries in the nearby hills. In time, twelve separate institutions were created, each with a leader of its own, but with Benedict himself as the guiding authority. The monasteries flourished, and Benedict—who by then had abandoned his cave—grew in fame and stature.

When he was about 50 years old, he decided to leave Subiaco and next appeared at the village of Casinum, 80 miles south of Rome in the Liri River valley at the foot of Monte Cassino. In the woodlands nearby, the people of the region had sacred groves and marble altars where Jupiter, Apollo and Venus were still worshiped. Pagan sacrifices were also offered in the citadel on the mountain above the town.

In the years which followed, St. Benedict converted the idol-worshipers to Christianity and built the forerunner of the famous monastery of Monte Cassino. It was here that he was credited with restoring the life of a monk presumed dead when a wall collapsed on him during construction. When a disastrous famine occurred in the year 536 and the monastery larder was down to five loaves of bread, his prayers reputedly were answered by the mysterious delivery of 200 sacks of flour to the abbey door.

But more important, it was at Cassino that he completed his noted Rule for governing the lives of monks and religious women in monastic and convent settings. This Benedictine Rule greatly lessened the harsh and ascetic characteristics of earlier regimens, and virtually revolutionized conditions for those who renounced worldly goods and pursued vocations dedicated to Christ. Pope Gregory praised the Rule, with its 73 chapters, as "remarkable for its discretion and lucidity," and because it was "conspicuous for moderation."

St. Benedict, for his part, was determined to make monastic life possible, not only for exceptionally devoted souls, but for those of less determination as well. Life as a monk, a cloistered nun or a community of sisters should be so patterned, he wrote, "that the strong may still have something to long after and the weak may not draw back in alarm."

At Monte Cassino St. Benedict was reunited periodically with his twin, St. Scholastica, known traditionally as the first Benedictine sister. When she died, she was buried in the tomb prepared for her brother at the monastery. Not long afterward (generally considered to be in the year 547), St. Benedict himself fell victim to a fever—or pneumonia, as at least one historian has opined.

Unique in life, Benedict was unique in death also. Tradition has it that, at his insistence, he was taken to the monastery chapel to assist one final time in the celebration of Mass. Supported in an erect position by his disciples as the priest offered the Holy Sacrifice, St. Benedict raised his hands heavenward and died as he stood with his fellow monks in prayer. As he had prescribed, he was buried with his sister, who shared his beliefs and his dedication.

Having professed his vows, Frater Martin returned to the classroom to complete his studies of pastoral theology, canon law and biblical archaeology with exemplary dedication. Meanwhile, his progress through the steps leading to ordination followed rapidly, and on September 14, 1856—the feast of the Engelweihe, an unusual celebration which occurred only when the 14th day of the 9th month fell on a Sunday—he received the Sacrament of Holy Orders. Officiating at the sacred rite in the Abbot's Chapel at Einsiedeln was Bishop John Peter Mirer from the neighboring canton of Sankt Gallen.

At the time, the candidate for ordination was seventeen months younger than the canonical age for the priesthood as prescribed by the prolonged Council of Trent (1545-1563). However, a papal dispensation was received from Rome, and Father Martin Marty—not yet 23 years old—was admitted to the cherished lineage of Christ's Apostles.

Unlike most Benedictines of his day, he experienced only two years of strict monastic preparation rather than the five or six normally undergone by the monks at Einsiedeln. Whether this weakened his commitment to the fine points of the Benedictine family spirit and tradition is questionable, although in later years, when he was accused of deviating from one of the Order's age-old religious practices, his departure from custom was attributed by some observers to the abbreviated training period.

Young as he was, Father Martin was quickly given heavy teaching responsibilities at the monastery. He was assigned to the fifth class of the Gymnasium shortly after he celebrated his first Mass on Rosary Sunday, the first major feast day following his ordination. Beginning in 1857-58, he took charge of the sixth or final class. For five years he taught in the Gymnasium, and as proof of his ability, one of his former students—Father Albert Kuhn, O.S.B.—wrote of him in later years thusly:

> "Marty was never simply a teacher whose goal was to funnel into the students a given amount of knowledge. He aimed to be an educator whose vision stretched beyond the confining walls of the classroom into the future lives of his students ... never was he slavishly tied to a textbook. His instruction was free and vivid. Just as he had wide horizons, he expanded those of his students far beyond the bounds of pedantic questions and answers."

Concurrently as he taught, his pen was active on various academic subjects. During his first year as a priest he wrote an essay of recognized merit on the methodology of Benedictine teaching a thousand years before his time. Published in *Der Katholik* in 1857, the treatise featured the work of Walafried Strabo, a contemporary of St. Meinrad, who was educated and then taught at the famed Abbey of Reichenau, located on an island in Lake Constance in Baden-Württemberg, Germany. In the essay Marty also exhibited his knowledge of the careers of Benedictine educators St. Bede, Alcuin and Rhabanus Maurus.

More controversial was his dissertation on the practicality of student associations in Catholic boarding schools. Father Gall, the rector at Einsiedeln and one of Father Martin's former teachers, complained that the organization to which the extern or non-resident students belonged was a hindrance rather than an aid to education. Its members, he felt, were manifesting a superiority attitude; they responded with insolence to the admonitions of their teachers; and they objected to faculty criticism of their school assignments, preferring instead the praise of their peers. In at least one instance, the association's publication contained material which, in the monks' views, "bordered on obscenity."

Father Martin, who himself had to fight a superiority complex in his student days, wrote in an issue of *Jahresbericht* that such associations, if controlled and properly directed, could have some value. However, he argued, if they were unbridled, they had no place in a monastery school like Einsiedeln.

"Youth cannot educate itself," he said, "[and] he who withdraws himself from legitimate authority falls into the hands of usurpers."

Understandably, there was strong reaction from the more militant extern students, but the views of Father Martin—who was not much older than the students themselves—were gratifying to the teachers who had to contend with youthful obstinancy which a century later was to manifest itself in outright confrontation.

Father Martin did more than write on the subject, however. He reorganized the student Akademie at Einsiedeln, associated it with the Sodality of the Blessed Virgin (which he had helped establish) and adapted the resultant organization to the needs of the monastery school. The Marian Academy, as it came to be known, provided an alternate to the student association concept and became a permanent fixture at Einsiedeln. Marty's legacy to his alma mater was based on its slogan: "True virtue, Christian piety and progress in learning."

Though his extensive knowledge, rich imagination and an obvious faculty for communication qualified him for a career as a Benedictine educator—possibly in the mold of the historically prominent monks about whom he had written—Father Martin soon became aware of a greater attraction than being a professor of rhetoric or director of a student academy. Pastoral work—the forgiving gift of the confessional and the power of the pulpit—offered a new challenge and a sense of fulfillment which he did not experience in the school environment.

As a student he had shown a talent for theatrics which drew applause from youthful audiences; as a preacher he abandoned all the tricks of the stage. As Father Albert Kuhn reminisced:

> "What he said and how he said it was of the greatest simplicity accompanied by very few gestures. Preferably he assumed a conversational tone—a tone of friendly dialogue with his listeners. This was more pleasing and went more deeply to the heart than scintillating, bombastic rhetoric."

At Einsiedeln he left 42 manuscripts of his simple, penetrating sermons. There is little evidence that his divided interests filled him with a sense of frustration in those early days. Instead, he applied himself obediently to the assignments delegated to him by Abbot Henry, who—undoubtedly recognizing the multiple talents of the young priest—entrusted him with the professorship of moral theology in the school term of 1859-60.

In far-away America, a time of impending crisis was beginning to develop. Abolitionist John Brown had led a raid on the U.S. arsenal at Harper's Ferry in mid-October of 1859 and was hanged in the public square of Charlestown, Virginia, on December 2. "Pike's Peak or Bust" was the gold rush cry in Colorado, and the discovery of the Comstock Lode in Nevada added to the lure of the West. Oil was discovered near Titusville, Pennsylvania, and there was great controversy brewing over a theory called Darwinism. Before the end of 1860 South Carolina was to secede from the Union, a harbinger of the fratricidal disaster to follow.

At a place called Yankton, some 800 miles above St. Louis on the Missouri River, a group of young opportunists had crossed over from Nebraska to occupy territory ceded by the Ihanktonwan (End Village) Sioux in the Treaty of 1858. Strike-the-Ree, the tribal chief known also as Struck-by-the-Ree, sadly informed his followers:

> "The white men are coming like maggots. It is useless to resist them. They are many more than we are. We could not hope to stop them. Many of our brave warriors would be killed, our women and children left in sorrow, and still we would not stop them. We must accept it, get the best terms we can and try to adopt their ways."

In 1859, while many of these diverse activities were going on, Bishop de St. Palais returned again to Einsiedeln to ask for more help in his Indiana diocese. The time had not yet come for Father Martin Marty, but the forces which were to shape his future were developing inexorably as he pursued his work with customary diligence in the monastery school.

Chapter IV

St. Meinrad: Up By the Sandal Straps

"... when beginning any good work, beg of Him with most earnest prayer to perfect it."

—The Rule of St. Benedict

While Father Martin Marty was growing in stature and knowledge within the protective walls of Einsiedeln, a prologue to the next chapter in his life was unfolding on unfamiliar soil in the United States. The progress toward a permanent Benedictine foundation in Indiana had been fraught with a litany of problems: personality clashes, drouth, sickness, poverty and misunderstandings. When Fathers Ulrich and Bede were sent to America in 1853, their limited mission was to assist Bishop de St. Palais in pastoral work and to reconnoiter for a possible site for a daughter-house of Maria Einsiedeln.

Once on the scene, however, Father Ulrich had other thoughts. In southern Indiana—about six miles south of the town of Ferdinand in Spencer County—he located approximately 2,400 acres on the west bank of the Anderson River which appealed to him as an ideal setting for a monastery. Without conferring with Father Bede or getting clearance from the abbot, he purchased the property for more than $10,000, mostly on high interest loans and with questionable possibilities of repayment.

This was the beginning of seven years of frustrating conflicts and heated interchanges between Einsiedeln and St. Meinrad's Cell, as the American foundation was first known. Mail delays—sometimes as long as several months—complicated the situation as differences were prolonged by angry letters which might never have been written had more conciliatory epistles "somewhere enroute" been received. Also, because St. Meinrad was in the diocese of Vincennes, Bishop de St. Palais was involved in some of

the decisions affecting it, and he didn't always agree with either the abbot or the monks at Ferdinand.

Added to that, the Swiss priests were unaccustomed to the humidity in the swampy Anderson River valley, with its flies, mosquitoes and malarial fever. Their first home was a two-room cabin with a roof so leaky that they slept under umbrellas when it rained, a far cry from Einsiedeln. Ironically, though, when their fields needed moisture in their first growing season, a drouth wiped out their crops.

Despite the early difficulties, however, in October of 1853 Abbot Henry sent Fathers Jerome Bachman, 56, and Eugene Schwerzmann, 43—along with four lay workers—to bolster the original pair. He was still sufficiently confident of the foundation's ultimate success that on January 5, 1854, he designated St. Meinrad as a dependent priory, with Father Jerome as its head. On March 21—the feast of St. Benedict—the priory was solemnly dedicated. A crowd of fifteen hundred Catholics and Protestants walked in procession from the church in Ferdinand through a chilly downpour to the farm where Mass was celebrated on the veranda of the small house in honor of the occasion.

Though he had been a capable administrator and professor at Einsiedeln, Father Jerome found it difficult to adjust to the conditions and demands of the struggling new community. He alienated the others priests—Ulrich, Bede and Eugene—all of whom wrote strongly worded letters to the abbot insisting upon the prior's replacement.

Shortly thereafter Father Eugene died of dysentery, and Father Jerome was recalled to Switzerland to give a first-hand account of the Indiana venture. Apparently he convinced the abbot that he was not entirely to blame because Fathers Ulrich and Bede were promptly rebuked by letter for their disparaging remarks about their superior. Nonetheless, Abbot Henry decided to replace Father Jerome with Father Athanasius Tschopp, 52, who left for America in the spring of 1855. He was accompanied by Father Chrysostom Foffa and Father Jerome, whom the new prior believed deserved a chance to redeem himself. As it turned out, this decision merely compounded the earlier problem.

Before the new contingent arrived in Indiana, the grist mill

(Opposite page): This first known photograph of Father Martin Marty (far right) was taken in the pioneer era of cameras. Identified with him in the Einsiedeln classroom were Isidor Hobi (far left) and "little Father" Fintan Mundwiler (second from left) who later were associated with Marty at St. Meinrad in Indiana. (Maria Einsiedeln archives)

and saw mill belonging to the priory had been destroyed by fire, and Fathers Bede and Ulrich were heavily burdened not only at St. Meinrad but in serving the neighboring communities as well. The three additional priests helped spread the work load, but the frictions—especially as far as Father Jerome was concerned—continued. Before the year was out, Prior Athanasius became ill with typhoid fever, and when the news reached Einsiedeln, Abbot Henry wrote discouragingly to Father Chrysostom:

> "And now this blow! The Lord . . . has shown us clearly that He does not will the work that we have begun there in His honor. It is my firm resolution, if Father Superior does not fully recover, to sell our whole possession over there as soon as possible or to hand it over to Father Boniface Wimmer [of the Benedictine monastery of St. Vincent at Latrobe, Pennsylvania], inasmuch as most likely no one of us would any longer care to take it over at his own risk and responsibility."

Father Chrysostom Foffa, four years older than Marty, was a "jovial giant" who preceded the latter to America and later joined him in Dakota for long service among the Sioux Indians. (St. Meinrad Archabbey archives)

Prior Athanasius recovered from his first illness, but had further serious health problems in March of 1856 which ultimately forced him to return to Einsiedeln later that summer. Because he was too weak to travel alone, Father Jerome was judiciously assigned to go with him, thus removing one of the abrasive conditions without further outburst.

In the meantime, big, jovial Father Chrysostom was placed in charge, on a "temporary" basis which lasted more than two years. Somehow he kept the pieces together, including operation of the priory school and the diocesan mission work, while back in Switzerland Abbot Henry wrestled with the dilemma of St.

Meinrad's continuation or dissolution. Weakened by malaria and affected in his performance by a propensity for alcohol, Father Chrysostom repeatedly asked to be relieved of his responsibility, a request which was finally granted in October of 1858, thus allowing him more time for pastoral duties.

Again a tactical error in personnel assignment created another rash of problems. Father Ulrich Christen—who deserved the credit or the blame for acquiring the property on which the priory was struggling for existence—was placed in charge. Neither his personality nor his relationship with Abbot Henry had improved. He soon generated new waves of dissension. Despite the burdensome indebtedness (much of it of his own making), he commissioned the designing of a coat of arms for the priory and bought a set of three bells—then he complained that he could not notify Einsiedeln promptly because "in all St. Meinrad I do not have 30 cents to pay the postage."

What brought matters to a head, however, was Father Ulrich's decision to schedule a profession of vows by several brother novices, even though St. Meinrad was not a canonically constituted independent priory and the abbot had not given his approval. When he heard negatively from Einsiedeln, Father Ulrich insisted that he either be returned to Switzerland or released to the jurisdiction of "some American bishop."

This virtual ultimatum was almost too much for Abbot Henry, who had already developed a plan of dissolution for the aggravating American venture. In the interim, another priest—29-year-old Isidor Hobi—had been sent to Indiana. Greatly distressed by the internal disharmony, he offered himself, by letter, to be the medium through which Einsiedeln could free itself of the priory without further harm if that were the desired goal. He would, he wrote, assume personal responsibility and legal obligation for all the Indiana property until the necessary arrangements could be made with Bishop de St. Palais, Father Wimmer in Pennsylvania or whoever could bring the matter to a reasonably acceptable solution. Later Father Isidor recommended that the abbot send someone from Einsiedeln who had full authority to act for the abbey—and his choice for the delicate assignment was a young priest with whom Father Isidor had entered the novitiate: Father Martin Marty.

The 26-year-old monk from Schwyz, by all indications, was being groomed for greater responsibilities at the monastery; but when Father Isidor's suggestion came from Indiana, Abbot Henry considered it seriously and then decided it would be a good choice. The trip to America would give Father Martin broadened experience, which might be of considerable value when he returned to Einsiedeln, mostly likely within a year.

Selected to make the journey with Marty was Father Fintan Mundwiler, born in the canton of Zurich a year earlier than his companion. Standing just five feet, four inches tall, "little Father Fintan" was an intellectual match for Father Martin, and both of them had delivered orations at the departing ceremony for the priests who first went to Indiana seven years earlier. Together they arrived at St. Meinrad on September 28, 1860, two eager, unselfish young men who—without knowing it at the time—were about to begin a lifetime of service in an adopted land. (Both were to die, prematurely aged and worn out, in their 62nd year.)

Father Martin, anxious to fulfill the mission assigned to him by Abbot Henry spent the first 18 days at St. Meinrad acquainting himself with the priory's spiritual and material status and began immediately to make reports to Einsiedeln. The priests of St. Meinrad were serving parishes at Jasper, Fulda and Ferdinand, in addition to maintaining their own foundation. At the priory Father Martin found nine brother candidates and eight other men who were either hired hands or elderly workers who did what they could merely for room and board. A secular priest, Father Philip O'Connell—who had been sent to the Benedictines by Bishop de St. Palais for "spiritual renewal"—also helped out. The inventory at St. Meinrad also included eight horses, 100 pigs, 80 sheep and 40 head of cattle.

With his facts in order, Marty set out for Vincennes to pay his respects to the bishop. However, the two clerics met unintentionally at Jasper, as the bishop—learning of the arrival of an authorized representative from Einsiedeln—was enroute to make his acquaintance and begin the necessary steps to resolve the situation at St. Meinrad. Their discussions revolved around various alternatives. When all the loans and obligations were totaled up, the priory's debt was $31,997.75—and that didn't include the $12,000 advanced from Einsiedeln on which not a cent of interest had ever been paid.

Bishop de St. Palais explained to the young priest that any hope of transferring St. Meinrad to Abbot Boniface at St. Vincent or to any other order was unrealistic because they, too, had all the problems and debts they could handle. On the other hand, the bishop did not want to lose the priory and the manpower it offered for him and his diocese. In fact, he wanted the monks to assume greater responsibilities in Terre Haute where both Irish and German Catholics pressured for separate services (a conflict between nationalities which Father Martin was to face on other occasions during his career).

The bishop offered to assume the obligations of St. Meinrad for legal purposes, with the secret knowledge that Einsiedeln would still maintain ownership. When Abbot Henry learned of the proposed maneuver to transfer title "on paper" only, he was strongly opposed because it smacked of deception. More than ever he was convinced that a way had to be found to get out of the American misadventure.

But as young and inexperienced as he was, Father Martin quickly recognized that "getting out" might be more difficult than making a new and stronger effort to persist. Out of the meeting with the bishop and further consultation with his confreres, it was decided that a small town should be laid out near the priory on land owned by the Benedictines. Lots would then be platted and sold, and the residents would then be members of a parish which would help the monks "pull themselves up by their sandal straps," so to speak.

On January 28, 1861—just four months after Father Martin had arrived in Indiana—the new town of St. Meinrad was officially founded. The sale of the eighty lots turned out to be a slow process, however. Because of war-time economics and the fact that

This early-day Benziger & Company engraving depicted St. Meinrad Priory as it appeared shortly after Father Martin Marty assumed its leadership. The frame church was built in 1858 on the site of the log house which had previously served the pioneering monks. (St. Meinrad Archabbey archives)

the buyers themselves were generally poor, immigrant Catholics, the real estate venture did not provide an immediate or magic answer to the priory's fiscal strain. In fact, some of the lot owners paid for their property by working out their indebtedness.

What the town *did* accomplish, though, was to give revived impetus to the foundation itself, and to convince Father Martin even more so that St. Meinrad could be saved. Concurrently with the platting of the town, the priory's school was reopened, with the ultimate but cautiously eyed goal being the establishment of minor and major seminaries for the education of Benedictine priests and diocesan clergy. By the fall of the year the new one-story frame building which housed the "College" was filled to capacity as Bishop de St. Palais took advantage of the opportunity to send all of his students to the Benedictines.

Indicative of his relationship with the see at Vincennes, Father Martin was invited to attend the provincial Synod of Cincinnati in the spring of 1861 as the bishop's official theologian. Not only did the role help Father Martin become better acquainted with the clergymen of the area, but through it he was able to broaden awareness of and interest in St. Meinrad itself. When he returned to the priory, he wrote to Abbot Henry on July 16, 1861:

> "... it seems to me that if God did not intend to preserve and use St. Meinrad, He would long ago have had occasion to drop it. So much good has been accomplished, so much sacrifice made, so much work done, and so much hardship endured that, after all, the blessing of God will surely come ... and make it into what obedience should have made of it in its very beginning."

Father Martin's position at St. Meinrad was unique. Among his fellow monks he was their superior as designated by Einsiedeln; but because it was expected that he would return to Switzerland by at least Pentecost of 1861, Father Isidor—who held title to the property and had taken out his citizenship papers—was nominally the prior as far as the public was concerned. This arrangement was generally well accepted by the other monks, except in the case of Father Ulrich. Almost from the beginning, he became a special cross to bear for his much younger superior from Einsiedeln.

In November of 1860 Father Ulrich—then serving the parishioners of Jasper—severed his relationship with St. Meinrad. Moreover, he carried on what amounted to a vendetta against his fellow Benedictines, reputedly advising creditors of the priory to call in their loans and generally causing unnecessary difficulties, not only for Father Martin but the bishop as well.

Father Martin called on the fractious priest to no avail, and the monks at St. Meinrad made a Novena of Nine Tuesdays in honor of St. Benedict in hopes of softening the heart of their rebellious confrere. Both Bishop de St. Palais and Father Martin urged Abbot Henry to recall him to Einsiedeln. (Unfortunately, Father Ulrich's stay in America was prolonged until 1865, and he left bitterly without making a farewell call at St. Meinrad. Later he continued to write caustically to acquaintances in Indiana until—several years prior to his death in 1871—he apparently mellowed and, as Abbot Henry wrote, "... he not only repentantly acknowledged his errors but as much as possible also made amends for them.")

Meanwhile, Father Martin maintained a busy schedule. He instituted the Sodality of the Blessed Virgin at St. Meinrad as he had done previously in Switzerland. He taught philosophy and aesthetics to the seminarians, and in a letter to Einsiedeln, he wrote: "I should be greatly mistaken if I were not the first and only professor of aesthetics on the western continent." Even more unusual, he taught the course entirely in Latin. He also instructed in piano and violin, although he expressed concern that the students should have a better teacher for the latter. He directed the 24-voice student choir and taught the art of preaching and dramatics as well. His achievements and acceptance were pointedly attested to by Father Isidor in a letter to Einsiedeln early in 1862:

> "Father Martin takes care ... of the parish at Fulda and once a month visits the parishes at Cannelton and at Tell City ... He does much that cannot all be put down on paper, cannot be expressed in words. His very appearance makes a deep impression: his modesty on the boastful American soil; his wise silence in the land of humbug exaggeration and folly is a constant mission sermon. All love him very much ... through him our institute gains respectability and credit. What a loss his departure will be for us."

As the first deadline for Father Martin's return to Europe passed and he became more involved in the financial, educational and spiritual affairs of St. Meinrad, it began to appear that his mother's earlier fears of "losing him" to a far-away mission calling would be realized. He himself had not yet expressed a personal desire to remain permanently in America, but the chain of circumstances seemed to be dictating a future for him which Abbot Henry had not anticipated.

By the end of his first year in Indiana, Father Martin had arranged for the conferring of minor orders on two priestly candidates with full canonical sanction, a detail which Father Ulrich had avoided earlier with unhappy results. On January 26, 1863, Fathers Benedict Brunet, Meinrad McCarthy and Henry Hug became the first priests to be ordained at St. Meinrad. Later that year—with the priory school functioning well, although producing little or no revenue—Father Martin went to Terre Haute to open St. Benedict College there. Once again his responsibilities broadened his commitment to his task in America and cut another strand in his tie to Einsiedeln.

On his return to St. Meinrad, Father Martin took charge of the parishes of Troy and the Swiss village of Tell City. On Sunday, July 3, he made several sick calls in Troy. On the following day, after his return to the priory, he became ill, but still insisted upon playing the organ for High Mass. By Thursday his condition had

Father Martin's sojourn in America was originally intended to last no more than a year, but as his involvement at St. Meinrad grew, it became obvious that his return to Einsiedeln would be permanently delayed. (St. Meinrad Archabbey archives)

worsened and a physician was summoned. Three days later the 30-year-old priest asked Father Isidor to hear his confession and administer Holy Viaticum to him. Meanwhile, at Ferdinand, Tell City and wherever the news of Father Martin's illness had reached, special services and prayers were offered for him. In his behalf a parishioner in the town of St. Meinrad made a beautiful wreath of flowers which was placed before the replica of the statue of the Blessed Virgin of Einsiedeln in the priory church. By the following Wednesday Father Martin was well enough to rise from his bed, and on Saturday, July 16—the Feast of the Blessed Virgin of Einsiedeln—he again said Mass.

Though St. Meinrad's location in southern Indiana was only a relatively short distance from Confederate sympathizers south of the Ohio River in the border state of Kentucky, the Civil War did not have a particularly drastic effect on the struggling Benedictine foundation. The work continued with mostly nagging economic difficulties adding to the normal burdens. On one occasion, though, Father Isidor's name came up in the military draft. His loss would have produced a serious personnel problem at St. Meinrad, where his schedule of activities was matched only by that of Father Martin. Besides administrative, teaching and pastoral assignments, he was also the local postmaster. Several parishioners volunteered to substitute for Father Isidor, but when he reported for his physical examination, he was rejected as unfit, and so the crisis passed.

For two months Father Martin underwent a slow process of recuperation. When he was strong enough, though, he again resumed his weekend trips to Tell City and Troy, where he experienced one of the few war-related incidents which he deemed worthy of mention to Einsiedeln.

> "The foregoing night [October 16 in Tell City] my life was in danger because an attack on the part of the Rebels from the Kentucky side was expected. At night, at half past eleven, there came a platoon of about thirty men with a cannon that they set up alongside the house where I was staying. One could hear other cannons thundering at a distance, and patrols marched in every direction . . . I feared more for my horse and buggy than for my person: the Rebels are in need of horses; they would not harm a Catholic priest, though they would lynch a Methodist preacher."

Father Martin escaped without harm. After that he made little reference to the war or to the social question which brought it about. His concerns at that time were confined almost entirely to the needs of St. Meinrad and to the people he served directly. It would be a dozen years before he would become intimately involved in another national tragedy with racial overtones. During the final year of the war, the Benedictines built ten churches—two of stone, three of brick and five of wood. At Mariah Hill—referred to by a pioneer editor as "the deadest little town in Christendom"—a stone church was erected around and over the old frame building which was dismantled from the inside when the new structure was completed; there was no disruption of service.

By this time the thought of Father Martin's return to Switzerland was virtually abandoned on both sides of the Atlantic. His life's mission had seemingly been dictated not by men but by God. On May 2, 1865, Abbot Henry officially designated him as prior of St. Meinrad, an indication that he had relinquished his plans for him at home. The priory, too, no longer teetered on the brink of collapse, and Prior Martin was able to assist Bishop de St. Palais in a personal way. His subtle sense of humor was evident in his letter to Father Gall Morel, his former teacher, written in late 1865:

> "I experienced many an adventure and shared many a bump with the Most Reverend Bishop. For ten years he had not dared to travel through the adjacent Perry County . . . True, the hills are not as high [as those near Einsiedeln], but cliff after cliff, small valleys cut through by stony creeks, woody declivities and stony rubble are everywhere. Three good-sized parishes awaited for ten years the Bishop's Confirmation visit. The priest who is in charge of them had uselessly written letter upon letter.
>
> "Finally I volunteered to lead the Bishop through the Promised Land with our horse and buggy. On October 21 I had our hardy Sam hitched up, a horse the Bishop honored by calling him Bayard, 'who was without fear and without reproach.' We left Ferdinand after a good breakfast, taking our dinner along in the traveling bag. We were headed for Leopold, 24 miles away.
>
> "At the halfway point, we stopped in a deep, wooded ravine, skyward-reaching trees above us, and the rock-ribbed earth beneath us, and refreshed ourselves with a few choice pieces of turkey, bread and a bottle of Catawba. We gave the remaining bread to our Sam, and, to strengthen him still more for his hardships, we at first poured some wine on it; but, as often as we offered it to him he shook his head and turned away from it, which was of great edification to us."

In October of 1866 Bishop de St. Palais requested that Prior Martin accompany him to the Second Plenary Council of Baltimore. There, as one of 120 theologians in attendance, he was particularly involved in the drafting of the decree which called for a broader use and acceptance of the Gregorian chant by both clergymen and lay people. During the course of the two-week council—attended by seven archbishops, 38 bishops and three abbots—he was presented with attractive opportunities to establish Benedictine foundations in Maryland and Iowa. "It is a pity," he wrote, "that I could not accept."

There was still work to do at St. Meinrad, but the odds were no longer so deflating. By the end of 1867, the priory's debt had been reduced to $19,265.24. Both the school and the farm showed slim profits which totaled $1,371.38. It wasn't much, but after 14 years it seemed that Einsiedeln's worrisome American experiment had finally turned the corner.

Chapter V

A Prior Lost, An Abbot Gained

"You must first of all learn English; you must learn to eat tomatoes; and you must learn to mind your own business. That's American."

—Father Isidor Hobi

With the Civil War behind them and the promise of permanency for St. Meinrad on the horizon, Prior Martin and his associates entered into what might be called a shoring up period. The earlier economic crises which regularly threatened disaster had been survived, and the time had come to strengthen and expand the priory's spiritual activities.

The seminary had quickly developed as more of a benefit for Bishop de St. Palais and his diocese than for the Benedictines themselves. Prior Martin finally had to tell the bishop that tuition would have to be increased and paid in advance for all of his students. The response from Vincennes tartly noted that under the circumstances of the ultimatum, he would simply remove all his seminarians from St. Meinrad and find new schools for them. This, of course, did not particularly disturb Prior Martin because departure of the diocesan students would permit greater emphasis on a purely monastic program.

As it turned out, Bishop de St. Palais discovered that other seminaries would be equally or more expensive, so he shifted to a conciliatory mood and informed Prior Martin that he would pay the price for any of his students who preferred to remain at St. Meinrad. Most of the German-speaking seminarians did just that, although several went elsewhere, especially after the prior issued a rule that smoking would no longer be tolerated.

Prior Martin's growing confidence was reflected in his readiness to impose new conditions at St. Meinrad, and although Bishop de St. Palais reacted negatively at first, the relationship between the diocese and the priory seemed to be strengthened rather than weakened by the increasing stature of the Benedictine foundation.

Meanwhile, Marty had added a new dimension to the work at St. Meinrad. In 1867 he approved the purchase of a small printing press and several cases of type for $450. While this did not result in an immediate flurry of religious publications, it was the beginning of an activity which was to develop into the renowned Abbey Press of later years. From his early days at Einsiedeln, the prior had shown great interest in the printed word. During the Civil War—before St. Meinrad became a priory—he had begun what was described as "a rather bold literary project." Because he was convinced that enthusiasm in Europe for the missionary service in America was dampened by a lack of knowledge of the Catholic Church in the United States, he proposed to issue four or more volumes in which the Benedictines at St. Meinrad would translate into German the works of various New World Catholic writers. Abbot Henry agreed to the ambitious endeavor and the first book was published in 1864. Though it was well accepted and set the stage for later volumes, only the one 518-page book was completed. Abbot Henry became concerned about the cost and the idea was abandoned.

Two years later—after he had returned home from the Plenary Council at Baltimore—Prior Martin personally entered into another publishing venture. To advance the council's decree regarding the Gregorian chant, he composed two books—one for singers and one for organists—containing ten Masses in Gregorian melodies, along with a bilingual introduction. The two volumes were printed in 1869 from plates stereotyped at the Franklin Type Foundry in Cincinnati. Though the harmonization they contained had some deficiencies as noted by later critics, the books themselves demonstrated Marty's range of talent and a personal compulsion "to get things done."

As the decade of the 1860s drew to a close, the priory in southern Indiana had evolved from a struggling vanguard of a few monks tied closely to a motherhouse in Switzerland to an institution which no longer had to rely on the beneficence and guidance of Einsiedeln for its survival. Through Father Martin, his appointed agent, Abbot Henry had directed the development as best he could at so great a distance. All too often, however, decisions had to be made quickly on the scene when transoceanic correspondence proved detrimental to the needs of the moment.

Prior Martin's obvious success at St. Meinrad led quickly to consideration of the next step: elevation of the foundation to the status of an abbey, an independent monastery like Einsiedeln itself. Abbot Boniface Wimmer, who had already achieved that goal for St. Vincent at Latrobe, Pennsylvania, discussed the advantages of an abbey over a priory with Marty during the Plenary Council in Baltimore. It was food for thought, but the 33-year-old prior, who still cherished a filial tie to his Swiss monastic beginnings, was not immediately convinced that the time had come for such a giant stride. Abbot Boniface, who envisioned an abbey at St. Meinrad allied with his American Cassinese Congregation of Benedictines, persisted by writing to Prior Martin after the council:

> "We are sincerely glad to hear from all sides that your Priory has developed into so flourishing a state ... that you must give thought to having it raised to the status of an abbey and that likely only your humility has prevented you from petitioning the Apostolic See to that effect ... The Abbot can do more than the Prior. I should therefore like to counsel you not to carry your modesty too far ... to the detriment of the Order."

Marty sent the letter on to Abbot Henry without comment. However, the seeds had been sown, and at Einsiedeln—where there was still some thought of a possible refuge in America if anti-monastic attitudes grew—there was favorable disposition toward a new role for St. Meinrad. Abbot Henry lightheartedly referred to the burden of his office as "abbatial lice" in a reply to Prior Martin, whom, he suggested, might also become infested with the same aggravating problem if the change were made. Nonetheless, he proposed that the monks in Indiana seriously consider the matter from all angles, express their preference and then the matter could be pursued in Rome. The resultant decision which Prior Martin communicated back to the abbot was that he and his associates were ready for the change in status—but that they preferred affiliation with a Swiss-American Congregation rather than Abbot Boniface's Cassinese group. That way, at least, some relationship would be retained with Einsiedeln.

It was finally agreed that the petition for elevation of St. Meinrad should be presented during a Vatican council to be convened on December 8, 1869. At first Prior Martin had not intended to go to Rome, but when it developed that Bishop de St. Palais would probably speak against the proposal, Marty changed his mind. He sailed from New York on October 16, 1869, on the French steamer *Lafayette,* intent on countering the objections of the bishop who, it seemed, feared the loss of authority to utilize the priests of St. Meinrad in his diocese if an abbey were created.

Father Martin went first to Switzerland where he enjoyed a happy reunion with his parents and relatives in Schwyz. Three brothers and three sisters had survived to adulthood. One brother, Father John Baptist Marty, had already been ordained, while Anton and Martin (not to be confused with Prior Martin whose baptismal name was Alois) were to follow in the same footsteps in 1870 and 1877, respectively. Joining in the homecoming festivities, too, were Magdalena, wife of Joseph Anderruethi, a sawmill operator; Mary Ann, who married Leodegar Stutz, a master shoemaker like his father-in-law; and Katherine Barbara, who remained single throughout her lifetime, devoting herself in service to her parents and her priestly brothers.

At Einsiedeln Prior Martin reported on the success of St. Meinrad to the assembled chapter of monks; and on November 11—the feast day of St. Martin, his patron—he was celebrant of High Mass at the abbey. While he renewed his acquaintance with his beloved Switzerland, he preached at Menzingen, Walchwil, Eschenbach and Steinerberg, enjoying to the fullest his homeland visit which included also the Christmas season. Then, in February of 1870, he was summoned to Rome to present his arguments for the proposed change at St. Meinrad.

It was a momentous year, not only for the Benedictines in Indiana, but for the Catholic Church in general. Pope Pius IX proclaimed the doctrine of papal infallibility; and then, when the Franco-German War precipitated the withdrawal of the French garrison which maintained papal control of Rome, Italian troops took over the city on September 20. Despite the fact that turmoil reigned and the pope considered himself a prisoner within the Vatican, ten days later he affixed the seal of St. Peter's ring to the parchment document which officially created the Abbey of St. Meinrad half a world away.

Notification went from Rome to Einsiedeln and then to Indiana where the good news was received by Prior Martin. Sadly enough, mail which arrived from Europe a few days earlier had brought word that his father had died on October 15. With mixed emotions Marty traveled to Vincennes to arrange with Bishop de St. Palais to set a date for the election of an abbot. In ill health following his return from Europe, the bishop did not at first accept the report with the same joy which had greeted its arrival at St. Meinrad. However, he had been delegated by the Holy See to preside over the election, so with seeming reluctance, he finally agreed to conduct the voting on January 23, 1871.

On the assigned date, following a Pontifical High Mass of the Holy Spirit at St. Meinrad, he assembled the fourteen Benedictines entitled to cast ballots. Four of them—Fathers Martin Marty, Wolfgang Schlumpf, Isidor Hobi and Fintan Mundwiler—had transferred their vows of stability from Einsiedeln to the new monastery. Newly professed were Fathers Benedict Brunet, Meinrad Maria McCarthy, Henry Hug, Fidelis Maute, Placidus Zarn and Benno Gerber, and Fraters Maurus Helfrich, Boniface Dilger, Jerome Hund and Athanasius Rumig. Fathers Bede O'Connor, Chrysostom Foffa and Eberhard Stadler, who chose not to cut their direct ties to Einsiedeln, were non-voting participants.

When the first ballot was cast, Martin Marty received all but one vote (his own), and a new chapter in his life and that of St. Meinrad had begun!

The new abbot, eleven days past his 37th birthday, immediately granted full chapter rights to Fathers Bede, Chrysostom and Eberhard despite their filial bond to Einsiedeln. Following appropriate ceremonies and prayers in the chapel, the confreres gathered for a meal of celebration at which Bishop de St. Palais—who had been at different times ally and antagonist—proposed a toast to the new abbot, concluding with the words: "The welfare of St. Meinrad is also the welfare of the diocese, and the joy of this community will ever be the joy of the bishop of Vincennes."

And then an unforeseen complication developed.

The original notification from Abbot Henry had verified the elevation of St. Meinrad to abbey status under the Rule of St. Benedict in affiliation with a still-to-be-established Swiss-American Congregation. He further informed the monks in Indiana that, in a departure from normal procedure by the Holy See, they could elect their own leader—which they had done. However, because of the hectic situation in Rome at the time, an additional notice that Pope Pius IX would *appoint* the new abbot had gone undelivered for four months. When it was finally received at Einsiedeln, Abbot Henry hurriedly relayed it to Indiana with a frantic message to stop the election because a choice had already been made. The situation could have been both embarrassing and disheartening to the small, exuberant community in America, but fortunately, there was a happy conclusion. The pope's choice was merely a confirmation of the chapter balloting. He, too, selected Father Martin Marty as first abbot of the new abbey at St. Meinrad.

The solemn blessing of Abbot Marty took place on May 21, 1871. Bishop de St. Palais, Abbot Boniface Wimmer and Abbot

Benedict of the Trappist abbey at Gethsemani, Kentucky, were on hand for the formal rites and the informal festivities which followed. After the religious ceremony, Father Chrysostom led the throng of parishioners gathered around the church in a mighty cheer for the new abbot. Bells and cannons added to the gala spirit. A collection was taken up, amounting to some $500—matched by a similar sum from the abbey—to be sent to the pope in his "imprisioned" status under the Italian regime. Father Isidor made an impromptu humorous speech, and Abbot Martin responded with gratitude for the show of loyalty and devotion.

Father Chrysostom, anxious to have his abbot properly vested for the historic event, earlier had written to Abbot Henry in his most charming style as an effective, amiable beggar:

> "... you will give your daughter [St. Meinrad Abbey] a fine dowry, won't you? It is true that the new abbot has prospects for plenty of crosses, but all the same, he would accept a golden one from you. Nor does he have a ring, crosier, miter or slippers. Truthfully, he has little else in his strongbox except hope and confidence in God ... Have I hinted enough? If not, let me know and I can turn on a little more steam."

No more steam was needed. From Einsiedeln came an antique crosier originally used at the old Abbey of Rheinau; an exquisite pectoral cross, decorated with semiprecious stones, a relic of St. Meinrad himself; a miter artistically festooned with needlework depicting the Blessed Virgin and St. Martin; pontifical stockings, gloves and slippers; two rings; various items of vestment; and other miscellaneous gifts. Disappointingly, though, the shipment didn't arrive until the May 21st celebration was only a happy memory.

✠ ✠ ✠

Shortly after his election, Abbot Martin announced that Father Fintan Mundwiler, his cohort of earlier days at Einsiedeln, would be prior of the new abbey, and that Father Wolfgang Schlumpf, who had volunteered for service in America in 1862, would be subprior. It was a good combination of teacher and manager. Father Wolfgang, in addition, was to take charge of a building program which would transform St. Meinrad from its flimsy wooden beginning to brick-and-stone permanency.

Construction of an appropriate monastic abode was given high priority, and plans drawn earlier by Father Bede were dusted off and assigned to the builders. Financial support came in the form of contributions and loans from Europe and the gift of a sizable coin collection from Einsiedeln which Abbot Martin sold to provide ready cash. Most of the material for the imposing structure was available on or near the monks' property. Sandstone was at Monte Cassino close by; 1,200,000 bricks were fired in the monastery kiln; mortar was produced from limestone hauled from a site near Ferdinand, while sand came from the Anderson River; trees from the neighborhood provided the lumber. It was a gigantic undertaking, but with Father Wolfgang cracking the whip (and praying incessantly), the first evidences of the four-story, fortress-like edifice began to appear.

On May 2, 1872, Abbot Martin blessed the first foundation stone. Four months later—on September 14—Bishop de St. Palais celebrated a Pontifical High Mass on a temporary outdoor altar and officiated at the laying of the cornerstone before a large crowd representing all the parishes served by the monks of St. Meinrad. At noon on December 19, 1873, a cannon blast signalled that the last stone had been laid on the majestic main building which, by its very appearance, announced to the world that the Benedictines from Einsiedeln were in America to stay.

Having delegated authority for the building project to Father Wolfgang and much of the internal administrative work to Prior Fintan, Abbot Martin devoted considerable time and attention to the abbey's school, to literary pursuits and to the spiritual practices at St. Meinrad. In addition to an extensive correspondence, he contributed periodically to the *Annals of the Propagation of the Faith,* wrote choral arrangements and instructions for the monastic choir, and authored a small book entitled *St. Benedict and His Order,* designed to foster vocations and generate enthusiasm for the work of existing and future monasteries in America.

He believed strongly in the opportunities for expansion of religious effort in the United States, and even before he had shaped the activities and facilities at St. Meinrad to his liking, he was looking beyond his own monastery walls. This was clearly evident in a letter he wrote to his friend, Father Frowin Conrad, a monk at Engelberg in Switzerland and a former classmate at Einsiedeln:

> "The West toward which the modern immigration of nations is moving is an ideal location for Benedictine settlements and there is a great future for our Order."

Seemingly, there was a restlessness within him, an inability to settle back and—within the confines of his vows—to enjoy the fruits of his labors. As his mind had extended out beyond Einsiedeln in his earlier years, it was beginning to reach out again from St. Meinrad.

This sketch of a stern-faced Martin Marty was the work of Father Thaddäus Zingg, O.S.B., and appeared in the German-language biography of the missionary bishop by Father Ildefons Betschart.

Chapter VI

No Cross, No Crown

"Happy would I be if I could sacrifice to God what Custer threw away to the world."

—Abbot Martin Marty, 1877

In some ways Abbot Martin Marty was an enigma. He could be friendly and warm on occasion, cold and cutting at other times. He was a humble monk, but in his position of leadership, he could be autocratic and forceful, too. Intensely devoted to the traditions of St. Benedict and the teachings and liturgical practices of the Roman Catholic Church, he could, conversely, depart from customary procedures to fit what he considered the needs of the moment. Though he was not a robust man, he was capable of pushing himself to rigorous physical extremes. Often quiet and seemingly shy, he could be a dynamic, effective preacher. In times of intensity, he found solace in music, in prayer and in devotion to the Blessed Virgin Mary.

Observers who wrote later about the early years of the abbey made a pointed differentiation between Marty the abbot and Marty the man. Father Caspar Seiler, a secular priest from Switzerland who came to St. Meinrad in 1875, sent a lengthy characterization of Abbot Martin to Einsiedeln in which he emphasized that "in his make-up there exists a certain inexplicable contradiction—a dissonance between head and heart . . ."

"During the first four to six weeks of my stay in St. Meinrad, my impression was that of practically everyone else who comes only into private, personal, friendly intercourse with the Abbot: I stood almost exclusively in wonderment of him, and I felt an almost mischievous joy when I thought to have found some little fault in him by reason of which he, as man, seemed to have some similarity to me . . . Indeed, the Reverend Abbot Martin makes contact with everyone with such a naturalness and cordiality, so much sets aside all ceremonial dignity, approaches everyone so understandingly, as man to man, that with the simple nicety of his demeanor and judgment he easily wins without exception the esteem and love of all who come into private contact with him ... And along with this there appear traits of so simple a humility, of so deep an ascetical, spiritual insight, of such a purity, and of such a nobility of pure intention, and above all, of such a ready will for sacrifice for a cause recognized as good or obligatory—a willingness that does not hesitate for a moment to make personal sacrifices, even those of health, of life and of the greatest inconveniences—that this esteem and love develop into a really deep veneration of the man."

But then the tone of Father Seiler's report changed. He told of seeing the Lord Abbot ill-humored and complaining bitterly, of speaking to the older Fathers in a cutting and sarcastic manner. The analysis continued:

"I noticed even more that at the examinations in the college he was from the beginning until the end only sour vinegar, that he dealt very coldly with most of the pupils ... and that he also treated the professors, especially the younger ones, like non-entities—an attitude that must have deprived them of all friendliness and confidence ..."

Supporting that observation was another report which told of the abbot's insistence upon seeing written copies of sermons planned by young priests. If he did not like what he read, it was not uncommon, the writer said, for him to tear the manuscript in two and demand a complete revision. For a man who couldn't abide mediocrity—from himself or from those he considered capable of a finer product—such a reaction could well have been possible. On the other hand, like many individuals upon whom the spotlight of historical retrospect has fallen, isolated incidents in their lives—good or bad—can be blown out of proportion with the result that an erroneous impression can be imparted.

Regarding monastic discipline and spiritual mortification, Marty's own ability to withstand severe privation made him a difficult taskmaster for those not so strong of body and spirit. He greatly restricted human comforts at the monastery, but he made no rule that he himself did not follow with rigid strictness. Father Seiler in his appraisal of the abbot concluded that the imposition of harsh fasting regulations had serious effect not only on the physical condition of priests and students but on their mental vigor as well. "The Lord Abbot," he said, "is too prone to throw actual frailties and sickly conditions—and legitimate needs and requests rising therefrom—into the same pot with effeminacy and unwarrantable seeking after convenience."

There were times when the abbot's strict demands backfired. After he ordered the wearing of the long Benedictine habit at all times, the brothers who worked in the fields complained that the unwieldy garment interfered greatly with their labors. Worse than that, when they perspired heavily in the heat of the day, the black dye in the material ran, staining their underclothing and darkening their skin. When the abbot joined them at work—ostensibly to prove that they were wrong—he learned first-hand that the complaints were legitimate, and thereafter a change was made.

He also had his position reversed on another issue which created considerable stir within monastic circles but which might be viewed by some lay observers as a tempest in a teapot. For a variety of reasons—among them economy and what he considered practicality—Abbot Martin substituted the widely used Roman Breviary for the traditional Benedictine book of daily prayers. The reaction to this edict was intense and far-reaching. Some of his own monks were outspokenly opposed to the change; and in Europe abbots of other monasteries decried the move as eroding to age-old practices which had given the Order its continuity and strength.

Abbot Marty, in turn, argued that "in a century of newspapers, telegraphs and railroads" the Benedictines could not set themselves apart from the rest of the Church. They should be following the same calendar and prayers which the secular clergy used, he said. Then he expressed an even broader concept:

> ". . . to be separated from the diocesan life and clergy would be tantamount to bringing about antagonism instead of community of life. To my way of thinking there ought rather to be a Benedictine monastery in each Diocese [as] centers of prayer and fountainheads of supernatural spiritual life. The secular clergy ought to receive its education from the Benedictines; with them, during its active years, the clergy should find recreation, renewal, counsel and help both for itself and, through missions, for its parishes; and into the monastery, the home of its parishes; the home of its youth, the clergy should be able to retire in old age or sickness . . ."

In the end the opposition to his precipitous action was so strong and widespread that finally the Sacred Congregation of Rites in Rome decreed that Abbot Martin was wrong and that the use of the Monastic Breviary should be restored immediately at St. Meinrad. The word reached Indiana on March 9, 1876; and on the next morning the abbot published the announcement in the

Chapter of Faults with these words: "What Rome wills is God's will and therefore also our will."

On the eleventh of March Father Chrysostom wrote a letter to Einsiedeln in which he described the resolution of the protracted controversy:

> "... in the evening [of March 9], after supper, Father Abbot joined us in the recreation room and, calm and composed, communicated the news to us. I must sincerely confess that at that moment I was edified at the demeanor of the Abbot. He declared to us quite calmly that he was glad that the affair had now been decided: 'Even though [as he said] so far as the liturgy and the seminary are concerned, one seems to have lost something by the decision; one has, on the other hand, also gained something inasmuch as by this same decision the belonging to the Benedictine Order has in a better manner been restored and more firmly established.' Thereupon the Abbot made known the resolve to re-introduce the Monastic Breviary at once ..."

Whether or not this "defeat" in a battle of ideas had a residual effect on Martin Marty's future career can only be conjectured. He made indirect reference to it in later correspondence—calling it "the momentary failure of our efforts at regeneration of the Benedictine religious life"—but there is no specific evidence that the decision from Rome caused him to turn away from monastic involvement and to seek new and less restrained challenges for himself. Nonetheless, in the weeks immediately following receipt of the decree from the Vatican, events and interchanges occurred which were to lead the abbot far away from St. Meinrad and into a new field of service.

On July 31, 1876, Abbot Martin debarked from the paddlewheel steamboat at the Standing Rock Indian Agency in a sparsely timbered land totally unlike his native Switzerland or even the Anderson River valley of Indiana. With very little knowledge of the Indian tongue or the tribesmen themselves, Marty stepped into a new world—one in which he would both succeed and fail, where frustration would run in double harness with his fervor.

The timing of his arrival must be remembered if the nuances of his first days as a missionary are to be truly appreciated. In the immediate aftermath of the Little Big Horn disaster, Lieutenant General Philip H. Sheridan, in overall command of the Military

Division of the Missouri, had begun a concerted reinforcement effort, bringing in troops from as far away as Missouri and Detroit as quickly as railroads and steamboats could transport them. Security measures were tightened everywhere, and emotions at the forts and agencies ran high. Almost more than at any other time in Dakota history the Indian was *the enemy*, and emissaries of peace and love brought a message which very few ears were then interested in hearing. Abbot Martin, however, was welcomed to Standing Rock by Agent John Burke, and he began immediately to acquaint himself with the people he had come to serve.

"The "Seven Council Fires" of the Sioux or Dakota Nation represented seven major tribal units speaking one basic language with three distinct dialect divisions. In their own tongue they referred to themselves as Dakota *or* Lakota *Indians, the name being derived from the word ko-dah or ko-lah for "friend." Paradoxically, the word* Sioux *originally had an almost opposite meaning, being a French corruption of a Chippewa expression for "snake" or "enemy." In time the word Sioux lost its earlier derisive meaning and came into general use to identify the people of the "Seven Council Fires."*

The Sioux were not native to the Dakota plains. In earlier years the tribes making up the "Alliance of Friends" were located in the Ohio River Valley before the more dominant Iroquois Indians forced them out of that region. In Wisconsin and Minnesota—generally between the headwaters of the Mississippi and Lake Superior—they again were pressured heavily, this time by the Chippewas (an Algonquin branch) who had a decided advantage because of firearms procured from the French.

Exactly when the various Dakota tribes and subtribes became separate entities has not been specifically documented, but as the Dakotas were driven out of choice hunting grounds by other Indians, various groups splintered away to seek new food sources, which was—and long remained—the primary concern of every social unit. The English colonies were already well established on America's eastern seaboard when the Dakotas began to emerge from the forested regions onto the open plains where—in their new environment and with the acquisition of guns and horses—they were to develop into a formidable power. In the Territory which was to bear their name they superseded

The Sioux Indians at Standing Rock Reservation, being enumerated in a census conducted by Agent James McLaughlin (seated, center), were the principal recipients of the missionary services of Abbot Martin and the other pioneering Benedictines during the era of the so-called Grant "peace policy." Tribal members at Devils Lake also came under Catholic jurisdiction. (South Dakota State Historical Society)

the earlier Arickara or Ree Indians, who had been reduced in numbers by smallpox and were no match for the more aggressive Sioux.

The tribes of the "Seven Council Fires" were the Wahpetons, Sissetons, Mdewakantons and Wahpekutes, known collectively as the Santees; the Yanktons and Yanktonnais, who were related closely by dialect; and the Tetons, who, in turn, were divided into seven subtribes: the Oglalas, Brûlés, Two Kettles, Sans Arcs, the Blackfoot band (not to be confused with a larger tribe with the same name in western Montana), the Hunkpapas and Minneconjous.

There was, of course, no mass movement of the Sioux into the region which was to become North and South Dakota. They came gradually over a period of years and by various routes, usually in pursuit of the animal most important to their survival: the buffalo. The various tribes and subtribes migrated to general geographic areas. The Yanktons, for instance, established themselves along the Missouri on both sides of the James or Jacques River. The Yanktonnais moved northward between the James and Big Sioux valleys as far as Devils Lake. The four Santee tribes encamped in the country around Big Stone Lake. Because of the nomadic character of their existence, however, it was impossible to pin them down to anything remotely resembling boundaries. They were free-spirited people, and they moved whenever and to wherever the hunting or trading called them. The various Teton bands were especially mobile, spreading out over central southern Dakota and ultimately crossing the Missouri to begin a century-long reign over their adopted prairie domain.

But then it all began to change. Fur-traders grew in numbers, and the buffalo became the target of commercial enterprise. The Indians cherished the guns, the kettles, the beads and other merchandise of the frontier opportunists and some even participated in the buffalo slaughter to acquire more goods. But the white man also brought disease and whiskey, sometimes further drugged with laudanum by the more avaricious dealers.

Ox-drawn freight wagons, stagecoaches, steamboats and railroads appeared on the scene; and before gold was discovered in the Black Hills in 1874, the Indians had been chastised, bamboozled, weakened by "firewater" and pressured into rebellion as their final recourse. Except for their startling victory over Custer at Little Big Horn and several isolated successes, their military effort was doomed to failure in the face of superior forces and arms, directed by men trained on the harsh battlefields of the Civil War and many of them seeking a belated return to glory.

In the summer of 1876—when America's centennial year was being celebrated jubilantly in other parts of the nation—there was little joy on the Dakota plains when Abbot Martin began to make his initial contacts with the bewildered and brooding people who had been caught up in a conflict of cultures not of their choosing. At first he would be involved mostly with Hunkpapas, Yanktonnais and Blackfeet; before his missionary service was to end, however, he would ultimately touch the lives of thousands in all tribes of the "Seven Council Fires."

There are legendary accounts of Abbot Martin arriving on the scene, bodily saving the life of the agent being set upon by angry Indians, and dashing across the plains in the saddle, his black habit flying in the breeze, to stop a heavily armed band under Chief Kill-Eagle as it was about to attack the Standing Rock station. According to a dramatic version written by Bishop John Shanley of Fargo in 1902, the climax of the tinderbox episode occurred thusly:

> "At that moment of impending danger one could see a solitary horseman, attired in the garb of a Benedictine monk, galloping toward the sullen, hostile warriors, who received him with great respect. It was Abbot Marty. In him they recognized the black gown, and their former love and esteem for the great missionary, Father De Smet, whom they had known, roused their savage hearts to better sentiments. They listened to Abbot Marty attentively, and, submitting to his fatherly advice and pleadings for peace, dismounted and gave up their arms, which the soldiers gathered up in wagon loads. Thus was peace restored through the gentleness, courage and apostolic zeal of that humble and holy monk."

That, of course, wasn't *exactly* how it happened. Abbot Martin couldn't speak more than the simplest Sioux greeting at the time, and throughout all his association with the Indians, he never completely mastered the language enough to attempt a sermon or major transaction without an interpreter. Nonetheless, his ameliorating, pacifying influence was soon felt, and in a matter of weeks he was accomplishing notable peace-making results without the Hollywoodian overtones.

The order to disarm and dismount the Sioux had aggravated

the already touchy situation. Without question, it was understandable for the Indians to be surly and belligerent; and although they were not a major military threat to the United States as a whole, they could—in small bands and as individuals—create continuing isolated incidents which might well have resulted in extensive bloodshed and property damage. Even though he was supposedly on a reconnoitering mission only, Abbot Martin began almost immediately to urge the Sioux in and around the agency to comply with the government demand. There is ample evidence that, despite language limitations, he was effective in heading off further trouble in the Standing Rock vicinity. Lingering memories of earlier "black robes" made it possible for him to approach the Indians in a way which was impossible for the military or civil agents because of the abrasive relationship.

As he visited the various camps, the abbot assessed the attitudes and conditions as they existed and concluded that the doling of rations had already taken its toll in the realm of human pride and ambition and would continue to be a major obstacle to resolution of white-Indian animosities. To Father J. B. A. Brouillet, head of the Bureau of Catholic Indian Missions, he wrote:

> "The policy of the U.S. has made these people a set of idlers, loafers and beggars, and as long as the military shall control them, it will be impossible to change their situation and character, no matter how good the intention of superior officers may be. It is not in the power of mortals to change the nature of things."

In his mind there was only one answer and it lay in the monastic Rule to which he was dedicated:

> "The conversion and civilization of pagan peoples was the task of the Benedictines at all times, and if they had stayed at it, there would not now be still 500 million children 'in darkness and in the shadow of death' . . . The *ora et labora* is today still the only remedy for healing the children of Adam . . ."

Despite appeals of the Quakers and other pacifists, the U. S. Congress was in no mood to cater to the Indians after the national embarrassment in southeastern Montana. On August 15, a Sioux appropriations bill was passed with the proviso that no further monies would be forthcoming to feed the Tetons unless they agreed to give up the Black Hills. About the same time Abbot Martin was formulating his own ideas on how to achieve lasting results through missionary efforts. His Benedictine background, plus his own personal ability to accept arduous conditions and tasks, were clearly evident in the concept he expressed to Father Brouillet:

> "... the main thing is to make the Indians work, and that can only be done if they have each his own homestead ... St. Paul's rule must be gradually enforced: 'If any man will not work, neither let him eat' ... To show the Indians how to work, I would like to get about 600 acres of land on which to build our monastery, and 300 in another place for the Sisters' farm and convent. I would have the Indians themselves build the boarding school for their children, the churches and their own homes. If the instruments are furnished, the carpenter of the agency and our Brothers can teach the Indians how to use them.
>
> "They never appreciate what is given to them, and education and religious instruction would never strike deep roots if they were offered without cost. You must either ask them to pay in some way for the education of their children or they will ask you to pay for sending them. There is not much nobility about paganism, whatever infidels may say or write to undervalue thereby the necessity or the benefits of Christianity. At any rate, one will have to take the Sioux as they are and be satisfied with small results in the beginning. If the alternative, to work or to starve, is finally set before them, they will submit to the former ..."

The fact that the 42-year-old abbot was thinking in terms of a monastery in Indian country so soon after his arrival in Dakota Territory is indication that he undoubtedly was prepared to leave St. Meinrad behind him as he had done once before when he left Einsiedeln for Indiana. Some compelling force—he would unhesitatingly have called it the will of God—had lured him farther westward, to a prairie wilderness of meager promise in wordly terms—but, from a spiritual point of view, a virtual treasure-land of souls to be saved.

Chapter VII

A Miter for a Missionary

"I must first save their lives if I shall save their souls."

—Abbot Martin Marty, 1879

On October 2, 1876, Father Chrysostom and Brother Giles joined their superior at Standing Rock. They lived at first in a one-room log hut with a leaky roof. There was a bedstead for the abbot, and mattresses on the floor for the other two. To fulfill their obligations as Benedictines, they arose at 3:30 a.m., recited the Divine Office, spent an allotted time in meditation and then Abbot Martin and Father Chrysostom took turns saying Mass on alternate days. Brother Giles was the server. The lone table in the room was their altar; on rainy days an umbrella was held over it to deflect the murky water dripping down from the sod roof.

As winter approached, the abbot viewed the enormity of his obsessive mission. In addition to the Indians on the two reservations assigned to the Catholics under Grant's "peace policy," there were soldiers and their dependents to minister to at Fort Yates, Fort Rice, Fort Lincoln and the other military outposts in a region larger than several Switzerlands. Moreover, as he assessed the area further, he could see that the limitation of soil and moisture would be detrimental to lofty plans of agricultural sufficiency for the Indians—even if they could and would adapt to a farming environment. From that standpoint, he agreed with those who were then suggesting that the Sioux should be removed entirely to more productive land elsewhere (possibly to the Indian Territory in Oklahoma) if they were ever to support themselves with plow and planter.

First of all, though, the language had to be learned, at least well enough to achieve basic communication. Father Chrysostom reported in a letter to Einsiedeln that Abbot Martin received his first lessons in conversational Sioux from a half-breed woman who assisted the Benedictines in their crude home. The abbot, in turn, taught her to sing Gregorian chant. Brother Giles, so much younger than either of the priests, adapted rather quickly to the language; and in later years Marty expressed an opinion that the Sioux tongue—with its multiple dialects—was almost impossible to learn fluently by anyone over 30.

Throughout their first winter on the plains they had to exist mostly on pork and beans. The cold was intense, and keeping warm was virtually futile with only wet cottonwood to burn. As the fire sputtered feebly at the back of their stove, water on the front of it turned to ice. Compared to their new existence, even the austerity at St. Meinrad seemed almost sinfully luxurious.

It is not unlikely that Abbot Martin thought of himself as a peace-making functionary between the government and the Indians, in addition to his missionary calling. As he acquainted himself with the broad picture of events occurring in 1876 and early 1877, he resolved to push himself into an intermediary role. In the wake of the Custer defeat, Chief Crazy Horse and a majority of the Sioux and northern Cheyennes who had taken part in that engagement spent the winter in the Wolf Mountains, unwilling to submit to the disarmament order despite the fact that the noose was being drawn ever tighter by reinforced U. S. military units. Another band—consisting of some 200 lodges under the Hunkpapa medicine man Sitting Bull and Chief Gall, one of the battlefield leaders at Little Big Horn—had fled into Canada to avoid the confining restrictions of reservation life.

As long as these splinter groups remained free, they challenged the authority of the government and were a continuing thorn in the side of the War Department. Because they were a symbol of the old Indian ways, their very existence hampered the work of civilizing and Christianizing at the agencies.

Convinced as he was that the ultimate military goal was the "extermination of these unfortunate people," Marty wrote to Father Brouillet, proposing to visit the estranged Indians in an attempt to convince them that they should turn themselves in before they starved or were annihilated. The Catholic Commissioner relayed the petition to the proper authorities, and on March 12, 1877, the War Department responded:

> "This department has no objections to permission being given to the Revd. Abbot Martin to go out to the hostile Sioux at his own risk with the understanding that he goes in no manner as an emis-

sary of the Government of the United States and that the military operations now in progress be not delayed, modified or altered because of his personal sacrifice."

An additional memorandum from the Department of the Interior, which arrived at Standing Rock two days later, said:

> "He will do so, however, at his own expense, but may take for an escort a few of the Indians most suitable for that purpose from your agency. The party may receive rations and such transportation as can be spared from the agency; but no other expense will be incurred on this account."

The abbot, meanwhile, was busy in Bismarck, organizing a church and school for white Catholics at that important railroad terminus. He was excited about his forthcoming excursion, and from the very room at Fort Lincoln in which George Custer had a year earlier planned his final campaign, Marty wrote to Father Brouillet that he hoped to be more successful than the ill-fated commander of the Seventh Cavalry Regiment.

Early in May the abbot traveled by steamboat to Fort Buford and from there to Fort Peck in northern Montana. If his trip achieved nothing else, he rationalized, at least it would give

Abbot Martin's meetings in Canada with Sitting Bull, the belligerent Hunkpapa medicine man, have been embellished in the re-telling. Marty did not succeed in convincing the Indians to return to the reservation, but his willingness to venture into the remote camp of the Sioux earned for him a reputation for courage. (Author's collection)

Catholics at the military posts and along the way an opportunity to fulfill their Easter duties. On May 18 the Benedictine missionary and his small escort party—including a scout and an interpreter—left the Poplar Creek Agency for the northward trek. It took them nine days to reach the camp of Sitting Bull and his followers in the vicinity of Fort Walsh; and although the abbot's reception was cordial enough, the resulting parley—which lasted several days—failed to convince the belligerent Hunkpapa that, with the depletion of the buffalo herds in Canada, his cause was ultimately doomed.

This first of Abbot Martin's meetings with Sitting Bull, while relatively unproductive in its primary aim, had a secondary result. Although he didn't seek the notoriety, the episode brought recognition to Marty himself. To venture unarmed into the camp of the rebellious Sioux leader was considered an act of high courage, and thereafter the Benedictine monk, who previously had been little known on the frontier, began to assume a role of increasing importance.

Sitting Bull, Marty learned rather quickly, had not been converted to Christianity as it was rumored. He was instead—in the abbot's words—"a savage pagan." Following his return to Fort Peck on June 8, he wrote: "Sitting Bull possesses the cunning of the redskin in a high degree and, if civilized, would without doubt have become an astute diplomat and a sly demagogue."

One somewhat dramatic version of Marty's mission in Canada implied that he was so exhausted by the ordeal that he had to be carried aboard the steamboat at Fort Peck on a stretcher for the return trip to Bismarck. Be that as it may, the historic adventure and its after-effects were soon put behind him as he faced the massive task of his missionary commitment with little help and an almost non-existent budget.

Unfortunately, Abbot Martin's enthusiasm for the work in Dakota was not generally shared by his Benedictine confreres back at St. Meinrad. Although Prior Fintan capably directed affairs at the monastery, having the superior away on an extended absence was not conducive to monastic stability. Following receipt of a joint letter from all the priests at the abbey, Marty returned to Indiana on August 14, 1877, having been gone for 13 months. He was promptly besieged with a whole set of problems and complaints, not the least of which was the questioned wisdom of continuing the mission in Dakota when there were scarcely enough men and resources to fill the needs nearby. No doubt the abbot recalled a similar negative reaction at Einsiedeln a few years earlier when the struggling American foundation had more detractors than supporters.

Though the monks were hopeful that their abbot was home to stay, they should have been somewhat forewarned by his activities at the monastery. Instead of setting aside his missionary aspirations, he spent what extra time he had in teaching the rudiments of the Sioux language to priests and brothers, as well as to several sisters from the Benedictine Convent of the Immaculate Conception at nearby Ferdinand. A letter from Father Brouillet requesting a priest and brother for the Devils Lake Agency at Fort Totten apparently excited him more than grappling with internal problems such as the drafting of specific statutes to govern life at the abbey as directed by St. Benedict's Rule.

After just three months at St. Meinrad, he disappointed his subordinates when he departed again for Dakota Territory on November 17. At Omaha, Nebraska, he met with Bishop James O'Connor, who then had nominal jurisdiction over much of the region demanding missionary services. The bishop had been unable to provide priests for the area, so Abbot Martin's personal dedication was a God-send to him. Accordingly, he named Marty his vicar general to fill the void, and offered him a choice location for a Benedictine foundation adjacent to southern Dakota in Cedar County, Nebraska, where many German Catholics were settling. Then the bishop directed the abbot's attention to an additional challenge.

At Pine Ridge, Chief Red Cloud, who himself was baptized a Catholic, demanded priests for his Oglala people rather than the Episcopalians to whom they had been assigned under the "peace policy." So, too, did Spotted Tail whose Brûlé Tetons were being relocated on Rosebud Creek. An uncle of Crazy Horse, Spotted Tail (whose name originally was Jumping Buffalo before he adopted a raccoon tail as his medicine symbol) reputedly had been instrumental in convincing his nephew to surrender after he and his people had run out of ammunition and were on the verge of starvation in the Powder River country of Montana. Crazy Horse himself was placed under custody at Fort Robinson where he died in pain and delirium on September 5, 1877, after being bayoneted by a soldier in a melee during which he had attempted to escape. As a result, some of his people fled to join Sitting Bull's exile camp in Canada as they were being led to their new agency on the Missouri.

As animosities were rekindled on the plains, Abbot Martin decided to see for himself what the conditions were at Rosebud and Pine Ridge. Indications are that he traveled westward on horseback from the territorial capital at Yankton. In the cold of early winter, he subjected himself to exposure and much personal suffering enroute. In December and January he visited both agencies and heard with his own ears the appeals for Catholic priests.

Protectively, Bishop William Hobart Hare, the pioneer Episcopalian prelate—who, like Marty himself, was often referred to as the "Apostle to the Sioux"—hurried from Niobrara to Rosebud to express regret that the abbot had ventured onto the reservation contrary to government policy. The Benedictine missionary was not forcibly expelled, but his presence was obviously not welcomed by the Episcopalians any more than the Catholics would have greeted representatives of other denominations at Standing Rock or Devils Lake. The competition for Indian conversions was keen and would continue to be long after Grant's unrealistic "peace policy" was finally rescinded in 1881.

Without going on to Standing Rock—where he had assigned Father Jerome Hunt to assist Father Chrysostom and Brother Giles in his absence—the abbot returned to St. Meinrad on February 9, 1878. Again his stay was relatively brief, and on May 19 he headed westward once more, this time with four Benedictine sisters from the Convent of the Immaculate Conception at Ferdinand whom he had recruited to establish a girls' school at the agency to complement the one previously organized for the Indian boys.

An incident at Bismarck—legendary or not—typifies the excitement and newness faced by the sisters who had accepted Marty's missionary challenge. As they awaited a steamboat for the trip down-river, they were at Mass being celebrated by the abbot. Midway through the service, they heard the shrill departure whistle from the wharf. Though the abbot could not interrupt the Holy Sacrifice, he dismissed the sisters with a nod and they scurried out of the chapel—with habits flying—just in time to board the paddlewheeler which didn't tarry for anyone. It was two weeks later before another of the infrequent river vessels came by to transport Abbot Martin southward.

The Benedictine women from Ferdinand, whom the abbot had known since their arrival in southern Indiana in 1867, were to be of monumental help to him in his mission. According to available knowledge, Sisters Maura Weyer, Placida Schaefer, Anastasia Sassel and Rose Chapelle were the first nuns to enter what was to become the state of South Dakota. Their pioneering lot was a difficult one, and in their reminiscences they later told of mice running along the rafters of their crude home and occasionally falling on the stove or into the cooking vessels; of dry whitewash flakes floating down like snow from the ceiling of their tiny church during Christmas Midnight Mass; of Indians, unfamiliar with liturgical etiquette, interrupting services by casually lighting their pipes with the flames of the altar candles.

Meanwhile, as the sisters were becoming accustomed to the frontier realities at Standing Rock, Abbot Martin continued his exhausting travels, complicated by the slow and erratic transportation of the era. In June he was at Devils Lake in the vicariate of Bishop Rupert Seidenbusch of St. Cloud, Minnesota. He was accompanied by Father Claude Ebner and Brother John Apke of St. Meinrad whom he had assigned to work there with the Sisters of Charity (the Grey Nuns), of Montreal, Canada, who had been laboring in the Fort Totten area since 1874. In September he was back visiting Red Cloud and Spotted Tail despite Episcopalian objections. The following month he returned to Indiana, stopping enroute at Omaha where Bishop O'Connor suggested that during the winter "when things were quiet" he should go East to solicit funds for the Indian missions. Though, as he admitted, he had neither taste nor talent for that kind of work, he apparently went on an appeals junket before returning to the abbey in mid-March.

On July 20 he left for Ottawa to negotiate with the Canadian

At the Farm School at the Standing Rock Reservation young Indian children were indoctrinated into "the white man's ways." Abbot Martin recruited Benedictine priests, brothers and sisters to staff facilities in and around Fort Yates. Men and women from other religious orders also answered his call. (Sacred Heart Convent archives)

government in behalf of the rebel Indians who had sought refuge in the "grandmother's land." From there he went to Washington, D. C., where he met with President Rutherford B. Hayes and others to determine under what terms Sitting Bull and his people might return to the United States.

The pace was superhuman, but there was no letup in sight. Instead, a further momentous development occurred. On August 5, 1879, a papal bull was published by Pope Leo XIII designating Abbot Martin Marty as Bishop of Tiberias and—in a subsequent directive—appointing him vicar apostolic of the Dakota Territory.

The news, which had been prematurely released to the press in late July, was received with great joy at St. Meinrad. The monks, it seemed, had lost an abbot and gained a bishop. Marty, meanwhile, had traveled from the nation's capital to Jasper, Indiana, by railroad and then by springboard wagon to Ferdinand where he paused to spend the night with Father Eberhard Stadler. When the abbot finally retired to his room, the excited priest sent a courier to the abbey to notify the monks that he would be bringing the bishop-elect to St. Meinrad early the following day. Then he quickly made arrangements to have his two-horse carriage gaily decorated for the trip to the monastery.

In the morning Abbot Martin questioned the reason for the festooned buggy, and so Father Eberhard confessed that the great news had been heard at St. Meinrad and that the Benedictines were eagerly awaiting their superior's arrival. As they approached the abbey, cannons roared a salute, bells chimed a joyous greeting and the town band came out to meet them. At the monastery the entire community was assembled at the entryway where Prior Fintan delivered an official welcome in Latin. After benediction in the chapel, they all gathered in the recreation room for a "family feast" and the abbot was conducted to a special throne, prepared during the night and decorated with garlands of flowers for the gala event.

But the abbot's intensive travel schedule had not come to an end!

Two days later he was on his way back to Devils Lake where he conducted a retreat for the sisters; from there he went to Bismarck, boarded a boat for Fort Benton and then traveled overland to Fort Walsh, Canada. At Frenchman's Creek he again met with the Indians in exile there, to tell them what he had learned in Ottawa and Washington, D. C. There are conflicting accounts of Marty's visit, especially as they relate to his association with Sitting Bull. Generally writers depict the Hunkpapa medicine man as the central figure in the episode, and that he and the bishop-elect had an amiable exchange, although no promise to return was forthcoming. Religious chroniclers often give the abbot credit for more success than can be historically documented, while an article in the *Yankton Press and Dakotaian* of November 18, 1879—shortly after Marty had returned from upriver on the steamboat *Big Horn*—offers still another version:

> ... The bishop knows Sitting Bull well. He is a passionate, opinionated and unreasonable chief who now has little power among the Sioux. Knowing this, the bishop cared not to see him and asked for the chief ... now having the greatest power.
>
> This position was held by Crazy Horse until he died in 1877 [after which] it fell to Spotted Eagle, a keen, intelligent and brave chief. The bishop met Spotted Eagle on October 23 and requested him to assemble together the chiefs of the Sioux that he might hold council with them ... Sitting Bull was not invited by the bishop ... as he knew the chief's stubbornness, and he didn't wish to show him any attention whatsoever.
>
> Sitting Bull had stated the day previously that he would not join the council, not that he had any contempt for the bishop, but he knew beforehand just what the bishop wanted ... In the council Bishop Martin arose and stated his mission. He came there for their good. He wanted them to be good Indians and learn the industrial pursuits of the white men.

Ironically, a successful buffalo hunt had given the Indians renewed confidence, and they chose not to accept the bishop's invitation "to come in and be civilized." Marty then told them he could do nothing for them until the buffalo grew more scarce, and they would be obliged to go into the agencies or starve. Although the mission itself was a failure, the bishop's prophetic statement, sadly enough, was to come true and ultimately force the exodus from Canada. As the newspaper story described the event, Sitting Bull appeared in front of the council wigwam but did not enter. He supposedly said very little, and when the meeting was over, he disappeared "without having received any notice or attention from the bishop."

Just which interpretation of the parley is correct remains as one of those unresolved historical debates, since Marty himself left no definitive report of the affair. After the meeting he apparently made a missionary call at the Poplar Creek Agency before his homeward journey. Then, shortly after his return to Yankton, he boarded still another train for the trip to St. Meinrad where his cherished monastic ties would be severed and a new chapter in his remarkable career would begin.

As deeply involved as Abbot Martin was in the Indian missionary field, he somehow managed to find time to pursue his concurrent dream of spreading Benedictine monasticism in other parts of the United States. Before he was designated as the first Catholic bishop of Dakota Territory, two new foundations—one in Missouri and one in Arkansas—were taking solid root, and in each case his influence was intimately felt.

In 1871 an anticlerical movement in Switzerland—generated partly by reaction to the doctrine of papal infallibility—again threatened the existence of traditional Catholicism. (Involved, too, was a splash-over of the so-called *Kulturkampf* of Chancellor Otto von Bismarck in Germany which resulted in extensive emigration of priests to America.) At Engelberg, south of the Lake of Lucerne in the canton of Unterwalden, the Benedictines were fearful of their future; and, at the request of his abbot, Father Frowin Conrad wrote to Martin Marty, his former theology classmate at Einsiedeln. The Engelberg monks wanted to know if there was a suitable place in the United States to make a new foundation in case a refuge was needed beyond Switzerland (the same motivation which helped sway the decision at Einsiedeln 18 years earlier).

Abbot Martin's reply was quick and enthusiastic. Send two priests to St. Meinrad as soon as possible, he said. He and his fellow Benedictines would help familiarize them with America and the opportunities it afforded, and then they could seek an appropriate site, using the Indiana monastery as a base. However, because the political situation in Switzerland seemed to improve, the abbot at Engelberg hesitated. On the other hand, his irrepressible counterpart at St. Meinrad, once involved, pursued the matter with typical doggedness. Additional letters followed his first, and one of them mentioned the potential donation of a large house, a stone church and 160 acres of land near St. Joseph, Missouri, which had been offered to Marty himself as a possible foundation site.

The procrastination continued for another five months before the Swiss community finally decided to send Father Frowin and Father Adelhelm Odermatt to St. Meinrad as Abbot Martin had suggested. Meanwhile, after learning of the decision, Marty quickly dispatched Prior Fintan to Missouri to accept the property in behalf of Engelberg. Unfortunately, by the time he arrived, Bishop John Joseph Hogan had given the facilities to the Congregation of the Most Precious Blood. Then—as the result of one of those happy coincidences which can be explained only as an act of

Providence—an Irish priest, Father James D. Power, was visiting in St. Joseph at the same time, trying to find a religious community to take over his parish at Conception in Nodaway County. In 1858 it had begun as an isolated Irish colony and had been struggling for existence ever since; more recently German immigration had altered its original ethnic makeup.

Father Power offered 260 acres of land and $1,000 of his own money as inducements; and Prior Fintan, unsuccessful in his first mission, decided quickly to recommend the second choice to the monks from Engelberg. Not wanting to waste any more time, Abbot Martin instructed his prior to have a small house built on the property as a temporary home for the Swiss priests when they would finally move to Missouri.

Fathers Frowin and Adelhelm, in the meantime, were being schooled at St. Meinrad in the language, customs and eccentricities of America. Abbot Martin also put them to work in Indiana parishes to broaden their orientation. Regarding Marty, Father Frowin wrote:

> "He has devoted himself to our affairs with an unselfishness which I have never seen before . . . Despite his many duties, which often keep him up until 10 at night, he still finds time to teach us English every day. He treats us like members of his own community and lets us take part in the community exercises—perhaps the best preparation for what we shall have to face."

The ultimate establishment and growth of Conception

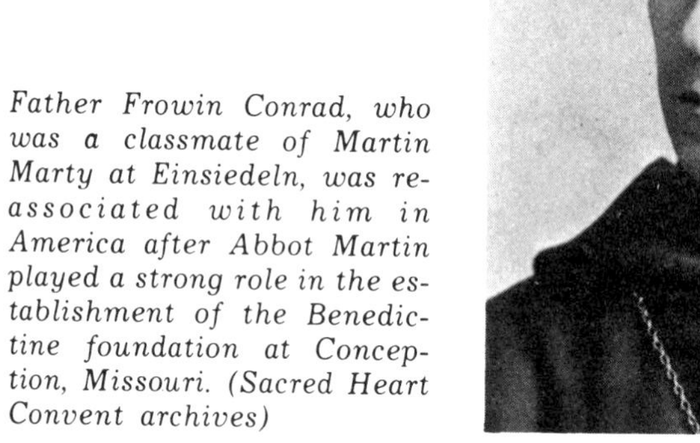

Father Frowin Conrad, who was a classmate of Martin Marty at Einsiedeln, was reassociated with him in America after Abbot Martin played a strong role in the establishment of the Benedictine foundation at Conception, Missouri. (Sacred Heart Convent archives)

Abbey—of which Father Frowin became the first abbot—is another story, but its relationship to Martin Marty and St. Meinrad in its earliest days cannot be overlooked.

Abbot Martin's involvement in the founding of another monastery was even more direct and, to some degree, heavy-handed. In the late summer of 1877 when he was returning to St. Meinrad following his first council with Sitting Bull, the abbot stopped in St. Louis, Missouri, to prepare an account of his experiences for *Amerika*, a widely circulated German-Catholic publication. The editor, Anthony Hellmich, was at that time volubly enthused about a proposal by Bishop Edward Fitzgerald of Little Rock, Arkansas and Col. William Slack, land commissioner of the Little Rock & Fort Smith Railroad, to establish a colony of German Catholics somewhere along the line. Hellmich, it is said, passed the information on to Abbot Marty who had indicated interest in the development of new Benedictine foundations wherever and whenever possible.

As a result, a definite offer was made to St. Meinrad through the abbot to establish a daughter-house in Logan County. On his return trip to Dakota in November, 1877, Marty again stopped in St. Louis to discuss in greater detail the Little Rock & Fort Smith Railroad proposition. He liked what he heard; and although his own abbey was burdened to the hilt with its own needs and those of the Indian missions, he promptly committed his confreres in Indiana to still another venture.

This shoot-from-the-hip trait, which was to get him into strained financial circumstances and numerous other problems throughout his lifetime, was also responsible for various lasting achievements which a more cautious individual might never have attempted. To move the Arkansas project along, he sent a letter to Prior Fintan, telling him to send Father Wolfgang, the subprior and penny-watching business manager of St. Meinrad, to Logan County to select the section of land which would be donated for the proposed monastery.

The letter—which arrived almost simultaneously with an edition of *Amerika* telling about the new venture of the Indiana Benedictines—was, to say the least, disconcerting to the monks who had had no opportunity to conduct a chapter vote on the matter. Differences created by the breviary controversy and Marty's rather independent plunge into the Indian mission field had almost been forgotten when this latest precipitous action on the part of the abbot reminded them again of earlier abrasions.

Dutifully, though, Prior Fintan sent Father Isidor to Arkansas

(Father Wolfgang couldn't go because he was recovering from painful foot surgery); and, despite his lack of business acumen, the priest-professor chose the site and signed the papers obligating St. Meinrad to the combination real estate and religious project.

Returning to his abbey in early February of 1878, Abbot Martin detoured through Arkansas to inspect and approve the hillside location selected by Father Isidor. A month later Father Wolfgang, Brother Kaspar Hildesheim and Brother Hilarin Benetz—along with two cows, two pigs and a wagonload of luggage—were enroute to begin a new adventure 700 miles away. After a litany of trials and tribulations, the fiscally insecure foundation—known first as St. Benedict's Priory—ultimately became the prospering monastery of New Subiaco, a name originally proposed by Abbot Martin himself.

(Interestingly enough, when New Subiaco became an abbey, its first abbot was Father Ignatius Conrad, a Benedictine monk from Einsiedeln, who was the younger brother of Abbot Frowin, Conception's first superior.)

While Martin Marty's direct connection with both the Missouri and Arkansas foundations ended with his departure from St. Meinrad for his vicariate in Dakota Territory, a filial thread always remained—and, in the case of Conception Abbey, an important epilogue was yet to be written.

Chapter VIII

Mount Marty: The Yankton Years

"You who are a monk ought not to desert the solitude of the monastery without good and reasonable motive."

—Abbot John Tritheim

Bishop Martin Marty, age 46, was consecrated on February 1, 1880, at St. Ferdinand's Church, Ferdinand, Indiana. Officiating was the Rt. Rev. Francis Silas Chatard, bishop of Vincennes, who had succeeded Bishop Maurice de St. Palais following the latter's death on June 28, 1877. It had been rumored at the time that Abbot Martin was on the list-of-three submitted to Rome to fill the vacancy, but apparently strong objections to a German-speaking prelate in the Indiana diocese eliminated him from consideration.

Had he been named to the see of Vincennes, it is unlikely that the monks of St. Meinrad would have continued to spearhead the missionary work in Dakota. Except for the personal dedication of Marty and a few individuals almost lost in anonymity on the prairie, the Bureau of Catholic Indian Missions was constantly frustrated in its efforts to generate interest in and support for the rigorous and seemingly unrewarding labors among the Sioux. As the Benedictines gathered with the parishioners of the southern Indiana communities in the church filled to overflowing, they heard the words which relieved Martin Marty of the dual role which had tugged relentlessly at his conscience from two disparate directions. With his monastic obligations behind him, at last he could devote himself entirely to his ill-served Indians as Vicar Apostolic of Dakota Territory and Titular Bishop of Tiberias.

It has long been a custom of the Catholic Church, in areas not fully developed to diocesan standards, to establish,

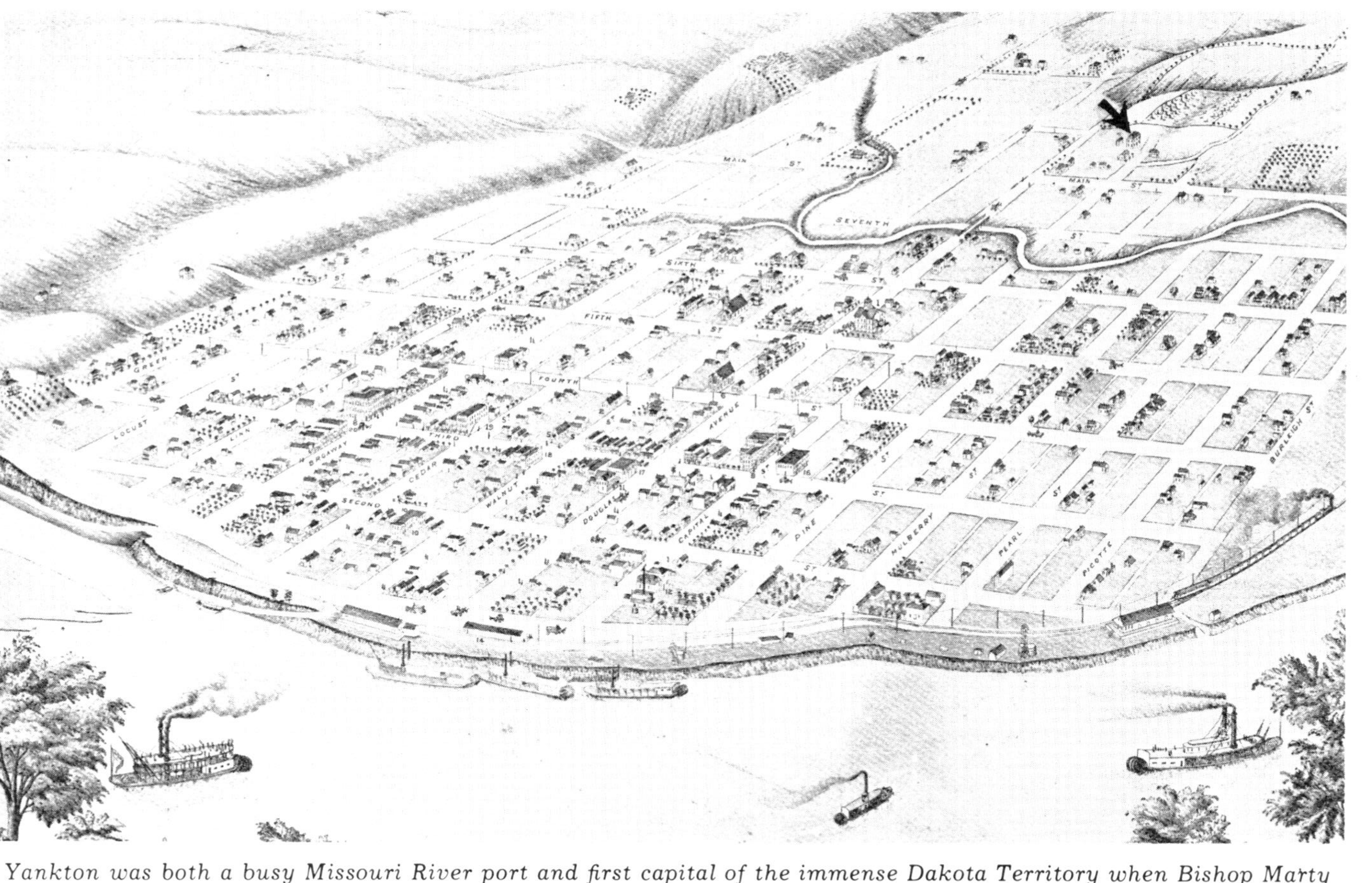

Yankton was both a busy Missouri River port and first capital of the immense Dakota Territory when Bishop Marty established his episcopal see there. This pictorial view, drawn in the 1870s, shows the bluffs on the western edge of the town, part of which became known as Mount Marty. The arrow in the upper right hand corner points out the combination house and chapel of Father Valentine Sommereisen, first resident priest. (Yankton County Historical Society)

as an intermediate stage, a vicariate governed by a vicar apostolic with the rank of titular bishop. Such bishops are assigned symbolically to an ancient city or see which had flourished in the past and then for some reason or other had to be abandoned by the Church. These so-called titular sees were instituted to preserve the memory of early-day Christian achievements.

Such was the case in Dakota Territory where Martin Marty, in the traditional manner, was designated Bishop of Tiberias, a city built by Herod Antipas on the western shore of the Sea of Galilee between A.D. 17 and 22. It served as capital of his tetrarchy and was named in honor of the Emperor Tiberius. Many Romans and Greeks settled there, some seeking cures in the medicinal hot springs near the city; and heathen customs abounded. In its history it has had both Jewish and Muslim eras; the Talmud is said to have been edited there. During the reign of Constantine the Great, Christians moved in, and in the 5th century there was indeed a bishop of Tiberias. With its pagan beginnings, the city represented a formidable challenge to missionaries and crusaders through the years. Centuries later, Bishop Marty's "new Tiberias" offered an equally challenging test.

After extending his stay in Indiana just long enough to ordain five new priests, Bishop Marty left St. Meinrad for the prairie hinterland and the work he cherished most. Already there was more to consider in the vast Territory than the Sioux Indians. The so-called "Dakota boom," which had begun in 1878 and was to last a full decade, was bringing hundreds of families into the eastern half of the region. Among the immigrants were Irish railroad workers, Czechs, Poles and especially Germans from southern Russia, many of them Catholics.

Bishop Marty's jurisdiction covered almost 150,000 square miles. It ranged from 300 to 370 miles wide and stretched northward from Nebraska to the Canadian border 420 miles away. As the crow would fly, it was approximately 460 miles from the territorial capital at Yankton to Fort Buford on the Montana border; but following the meandering bends of the Missouri, a steamboat had to travel more than 700 miles to cover the same distance.

At the Standing Rock Agency, the bishop would have been near the center of his vicariate, but for logistical and undoubtedly political reasons, Yankton was chosen as his episcopal see—even though the bishop himself planned to be somewhat of an itinerant prelate, being located, at least in the beginning, wherever he would hang his pectoral cross. The Mother City of the Dakotas had been founded in 1858; and four years later—when Congress established the immense Dakota Territory (which then stretched all the way to Idaho), the mud-bound village on the Missouri became the seat of government. Catholics, though a minority of the population, had built a large frame church in 1876, the year Abbot Marty had first passed almost unnoticed through the bustling river-front town. That church, for which the original bid had been only $1,682, was designated as the bishop's procathedral. The pastor of Sacred Heart parish—Father George L. Willard—was named vicar general in addition to his other duties.

Meanwhile, Father Chrysostom and the other pioneer missionaries were carrying on at the northern reservations, with more

Sacred Heart Church in Yankton was designated as Bishop Marty's procathedral during his stay in the Mother City. The foundation for the wooden structure was laid just a few weeks after Abbot Martin first passed through the Missouri River port in the summer of 1876. (Sacred Heart Church archives)

zeal and ingenuity than with adequate backup support. The "long winter" of 1880-81, with its disastrous blizzards, brought intense suffering to Indians and whites alike. In the spring the Missouri raged out of control, as jagged ice floes destroyed steamboats caught in the fall freeze-up and, for all practical purposes, brought to an end the romantic era of river transport. When the weather improved, Sitting Bull and some 1,300 so-called hostile Sioux returned to the United States from Canada, choosing reservation life to starvation as the lesser of two evils. Sitting Bull himself was incarcerated at Fort Randall some 70 miles west of Yankton where Bishop Marty would visit him again the following year.

On September 26, 1881, the bishop joined the territorial and civic leaders of Yankton at the local Congregational Church where he was a featured speaker at memorial services for President James A. Garfield, who was victim of an assassin's bullet a week earlier. Back in Washington, D. C., frustrated government authorities finally gave up completely on the ill-conceived "peace policy" on Indian reservations and opened them up to competitive missionary activity. For Bishop Marty this meant he could broaden his efforts among the Sioux—if he could only get the priests, the sisters and the money to operate new schools and churches.

If nothing else, though, he could personally visit the agencies, the embryonic parishes and even the individual huts of homesteaders and Indians. He traveled by every available means

Father George L. Willard, pastor of Sacred Heart Church in Yankton, was also Bishop Marty's first vicar general. A convert to Catholicism, he was in demand as a lecturer and also served as one of the editors of the Catholic Citizen, *published in Milwaukee. (Sacred Heart Convent archives)*

of conveyance: to cornerstone-layings, confirmation services, preaching missions and simple humanitarian calls. By sled, surrey, stagecoach and even railroad baggage car, he crisscrossed his vicariate—teaching, building and spreading the message of Christ. Wherever he went, he maintained his voluminous correspondence. Even as he traveled the back-country and camped along the way, he would sit beside the wagon with his writing pad and pen. He especially tried to keep Father Brouillet at the Catholic Indian Bureau informed of conditions in Dakota. On July 13, 1882, a letter posted at Chamberlain said, in part:

> "I left Yankton on the 5th inst. and am traveling along the Missouri River up to Fort Yates and shall by the first Sunday of August be in Ft. Totten to make my contact with the sisters. In Randall last Sunday I saw Sitting Bull and could not help feeling the deepest compassion for him and his people. Cannot you do anything at all to obtain mercy and justice?
>
> "You are aware that Sitting Bull would like to go to Grand River where the Hunkpapas since his time have made their home, buried their fathers and where there is plenty of wood. Those who do not know him are therefore suspicious . . . If people are afraid of sending Sitting Bull to Grand River and want to keep him south and near the military, then the most suitable place is . . . the former agency of Spotted Tail on the west bank of the Missouri River, 25 miles above Fort Randall with an abundance of timber and good soil. He should be located there this fall, so as to be in working order at the beginning of next spring.
>
> "If we are in earnest about the civilization of the Indians, things should be provided at the right time and in the right shape . . . Please do or suggest something I can do for Sitting Bull—they want activity and not words! Before I left the camp last Monday I baptized three sick women in Sitting Bull's tent, Maria, Anna and Felicity . . ."

Unfortunately, the bishop's rigorous travel and work schedule was undermining his own health. The reminiscences of a traveling companion, Joseph Helmig—who later served as a hired man for the sisters at Standing Rock—portray graphically the ordeals willingly experienced by the bishop and the toll they were obviously taking on him physically. While there may have been some discrepancies in his recollection, Helmig wrote:

> "During the last weeks of 1882 Bishop Marty . . . asked me whether I would accompany him on a wagon trip he was planning to make across the prairies . . . He told me he planned to make Standing Rock the end of his journey to spend the winter there, and that he was having a house built where we could live. I would be

the cook and housekeeper. I told him I could not do that because I knew nothing about cooking; he replied, 'I will teach you.' And teach me he did.

"In Pierre we bought two light horses and a wagon, a tent, some blankets, a coffee pot, two tin drinking cups, some hard tack and crackers, bacon and ground coffee, and some sacks of corn for the horses. Off we went across the prairies toward the Rosebud Agency. On our very first day we found that the horses were balky, and in dangerous places put us in peril of our lives. Here is an example:

"We had spent a night in a valley where we found some wood and water, something not everywhere available. We often had to use water from pools in which prairie wolves and other animals had bathed and so our horses wouldn't drink it. This particular morning the bishop was in great pain, as often he had a severe headache. He could not eat, and the burning heat of the sun made things much worse. I was afraid he would die on the trip—often he was as pale as a corpse.

"When we wanted to leave by the little-traveled trail leading out of the valley, we found it very overgrown and leading up a rather steep hill; a deep ravine skirted it on one side. I walked ahead, exploring the trail a bit. I let the bishop drive after advising him not to halt but to whip up the horses so he could make it in one attempt. I knew very well that if they stopped, those horses would not again go ahead. Meanwhile, I picked up a buffalo skull to put behind the wheel in case the wagon should slip backwards.

"What I had feared happened, and in the most dangerous spot. I threw the skull behind the wheel, but the horses backed the wagon

It was the belief of Bishop Marty, Agent James McLaughlin and many others that "civilizing and Christianizing" the Indians could best be achieved through education of the young Sioux. This policy was rigorously pursued at Fort Yates (above) and at other reservations after the "peace policy" was rescinded. (Sacred Heart Convent archives)

right over it and I had to push with all my might to keep [it] from going over the cliff. Had that happened, the bishop would surely have been killed and the wagon and horses lost ...

"I shouted to the bishop to jump down and unhitch the horses while I held on to the wagon ... until the bishop could secure it with stones. We unloaded everything and carried it up the hill. The bishop was totally exhausted, and from his looks, I was afraid he would die right out there on the prairie. After he had recovered a bit, I pushed the wagon down the hill. We hitched up again and drove around ... until we found a place where I could make it in one attempt. By this time the bishop was totally unable to continue.

"I drove back about three miles where I could get water for the horses. We then settled down to our third night on the prairie; it was not to be without further excitement. We took the seat and box off the wagon so the bishop could sleep on some hay ... and cover himself with a blanket. I slept on the ground wrapped in a blanket and buffalo robe. The bishop woke up first, of course, and was standing beside me ... When I wanted to crawl out of the blanket, something was holding my feet very fast. I threw back the blanket only to find a big black snake coiled tightly about my bare feet. Either I was its prey or it simply wanted to keep warm, I never did find out ... There was but a single comment from the bishop: 'Never again will you sleep on the ground.'

"After that we both slept in the wagon but could not lie on our backs as the wagon was so narrow. We could not turn at will; turning required previous agreement ... The bishop said: 'You are an old soldier; you give the order.' We could sleep a little, but real rest was out of the question, and the bishop's condition grew worse each day. He had neither proper rest nor sleep; then there was the great heat by day and the rather cold nights. Nor could he eat because our only rations were black coffee, crackers and dried bacon.

"On the evening of the fourth day we planned to set up our tent because the bishop planned to say Mass in the morning. All afternoon of that day we had noticed smoke at a great distance off to the right. We unloaded our belongings and were about to put up our tent when we realized that with the turning of the wind a great prairie fire was heading toward us. We reloaded, hitched up and the bishop drove off a short distance while I burned off an area onto which we drove our wagon to be safe from the fire. We barely made it! We had a terrible time managing our horses which were maddened by the smoke, the roar of the wind and fire, and the heat. All around us everything had been burned so that there was no grass for the horses; we had to go back several miles to an area that the fire had by-passed.

"During the night we had several inches of snow, so the next day dawned cold. Since the ground was not frozen, the snow balled up so badly under the horses' hooves that we had to stop and unhitch after covering hardly more than a mile. There was nothing to do but wait until it turned sunny and the snow melted. The same day we met some Indians coming from the Black Hills; they told us we were not on the right road to the Rosebud Agency. We drove back with them to the point where we should have taken off for the agency. On the sixth day we finally arrived at our goal without further mishap.

"The bishop had consultations with the agent, gave some religious instructions and conducted divine services for the Indians. The agent and everyone who knew anything about the climate told the bishop that under no condition should he dare to set out on his projected trip to the Black Hills; any day we might perish in a snowstorm. We made our way to a tiny railroad station—Valentine, Nebraska. The bishop went on to Omaha, and I set out for Standing Rock where, so the bishop thought, the house which he asked to be built would be ready and we could spend the winter there."

Helmig's account, whether embellished or not, points out the drain on the bishop's physical reserves. Yet, he did not alter his pace—he merely changed direction. When he finished his business in Omaha, he made a circuitous journey to Standing Rock where Helmig's memoirs pick up again:

"When I got to the agency, the house was not ready, not even plastered. Little enough did I know about plastering, but I did the best I could and plastered three rooms out of five, one for the bishop, one for me and one for the kitchen. I had not finished when the bishop arrived, but he decided to move in at once. Next I was initiated into the mysteries of cooking. The bishop taught me how to bake biscuits for the Indians who filled our house every day. I cooked coffee and baked biscuits from morning until night.

"The bishop had the largest room, and it was chock full of Indians every day. They were lying on the floor, on the bishop's bed or sitting on the chairs while the great-hearted bishop sat on a box and taught them about God. Often he had no chance to eat at noon. In the morning he offered Holy Mass in his room. When he had vested, he would open the kitchen door and say: 'If you are ready, you can come in.' I was his server at Mass.

"The bishop was more or less ill all winter. The house was not warm enough even though we had two stoves; the water on the cookstove was often frozen in the morning ... Lack of proper food was another hardship; there were days when the bishop was unable to eat anything at all. To top it all off, he was entirely too busy with the Indians; by evening he was totally exhausted and sick. He was always cold and suffered severe headaches. Especially his feet were cold; I put heated bricks in his bed and vinegar compresses on his head. Suffering of another kind also overwhelmed him. An event in Yankton stabbed his fatherly heart and caused his hair to turn gray within a week."

The episode, referred to by Helmig, which had such a physical and emotional effect on the bishop related undoubtedly to a news item which appeared in the *Yankton Press and Dakotaian* on December 29, 1882:

> Yankton has been considerably interested today over the marriage of Dr. V. Sebiakin-Ross to Miss Nellie Kerns. Dr. Sebiakin-Ross is a popular young Russian physician here and Miss Kerns has been known to the community and generally beloved, as Sister Mary Paul, of the convent of the Sacred Heart.

In a later era the marriage might have gone relatively unnoticed, but in 1882 the circumstances were decidedly different. The scandal hit like a bombshell, and the story went out from Yankton by telegraph to be carried by numerous newspapers throughout the nation. Taking advantage of the publicity, a local manufacturer named his best-selling Mary Paul cigar after the former nun, an action which perpetuated the unfortunate happening and grated on Catholics, lay and religious, for a long time.

While his vicar general, Father Willard, was intimately involved in the affair, Bishop Marty personally suffered the pangs of disappointment and a deep concern about its effect on his vicariate. As irrevocably committed as he himself was to his vows, he could hardly conceive of a priest or sister turning their backs on the Church. At the same time, the critical shortage of religious personnel to serve the growing population of the Territory was a constant burden to him, and the loss of even one teacher or pastor added to his problems.

The Sisters of Mercy—Sister Mary Paul's order—had come to Yankton from Omaha in 1878 to open a girls' academy. Well received at first, they appealed for public assistance and built a combination school building and residence atop the bluff on the western edge of the town which in ensuing years was to become known as Mount Marty. In the process they acquired a substantial indebtedness at high interest. As it turned out, neither the pledges from the townspeople nor revenues from their school were sufficient to bear the fiscal load; and when the scandal of one of their members weakened their standing in the predominantly Protestant community, the bishop stepped in to assume their obligations and asked them to withdraw from the city.

Fortunately, the unhappy episode was to have a fortuitous after-effect, by opening the way for another order of sisters to fill the void at Yankton. It was clear proof, according to many firm believers, that God sometimes works in mysterious ways!

From his earliest days in Dakota, the sedulous Benedictine

was continually seeking, not only more priests to serve the Indian agencies and new parishes in the Territory, but sisters as well. The Grey Nuns from Montreal, the Mercy Sisters, Ursulines, Benedictines from Ferdinand and the Sisters of St. Agnes of Fond du Lac, Wisconsin, were among the pioneer missionaries on the scene, but Marty did not relax his recruiting efforts.

He appealed to the Presentation Sisters in Ireland, and three of them—Mother M. John Hughes, her blood sister Mother M. Agnes Hughes and Sister Teresa McCarthy—responded in March of 1880, making their way to Charles Mix County. Their goal was to establish a school for the Yankton Indians and French half-bloods near what became the community of Wheeler. They underwent intense privations at their St. Ann's Mission before they gave up the cause. Then, at the bishop's suggestion, they traveled by stagecoach to Deadwood with the idea of working among the families of miners there; but when they discovered the rough character of the town and that there was no priest available for Mass on a regular basis, they turned around and went back to St. Ann's where they moved into a crude Indian hut.

When Bishop Marty came to see them, as the story goes, he found them living "among toads and lizards" on their muddy earthen floor. He promptly took them to Yankton where the Sisters of Mercy welcomed and housed them for 15 months until they moved to Fargo in July of 1882 to establish a foundation there. (Four years later several members of the order founded a convent in Aberdeen, southern Dakota. Through the years, from that focal point, the Presentation sisters developed impressive educational and health-care institutions to serve a wide region.)

For additional help, Bishop Marty also turned southward to Missouri:

> *On September 5, 1874, five Benedictine Sisters from the Convent of Maria Rickenbach in Switzerland arrived at Maryville, Missouri. Sisters Anselma Felber, Agnes Dali, Beatrix Renggli, Augustine Kuendig and Adela Eugster had come at the behest of Father Frowin Conrad, the Engelberg monk whom Abbot Martin had assisted earlier in establishing the new foundation at Conception.*
>
> *Later that month the abbot himself came from St. Meinrad with Sister Rose Chapelle, who had been among the first nuns to go to Dakota from the Ferdinand convent. He had assigned her to "acquaint the Swiss sisters during their early days at Maryville with American school methods and*

remain as long as necessary . . . until they have mastered the American language." Typically, the abbot had gotten into a brief controversy for meddling in the prayer-life of the Rickenbach sisters over whom he had no authority, but the matter was peaceably resolved before a major rift developed.

Meanwhile, three of the sisters were moved to Conception, 17 miles away, to open a school, while the others remained at Maryville. Though the details do not particularly have a place in this story, serious dissension arose between the two groups (and between Fathers Frowin and Adelhelm) so that the genesis of separate foundations had begun.

On November 1, 1880, Mother Gertrude Leupi, co-founder of the Convent of Maria Rickenbach, arrived at Maryville from Switzerland with four other sisters. Like Martin Marty, she had decided to re-direct her career to the needs of America. Her strong influence was immediately felt; and on November 17—a milestone occasion—St. Gertrude's Convent was blessed, and four candidates were invested with the Benedictine habit. (The occasion marked what has since been recognized as the birthdate of the community which later became known as Sacred Heart Convent of Yankton, South Dakota.) At Conception the other sisters, in turn, established St. Scholastica's Convent, with their motherhouse at nearby Clyde, Missouri.

Early in February of 1881, Bishop Marty—on one of his recruiting forays—stopped to see Mother Gertrude at Maryville. In the course of his visit, he outlined graphically and convincingly to the sisters the opportunities available to them to extend God's Kingdom among the Sioux Indians in his vicariate. Mother Gertrude and her associates accepted the challenge, and in July of that same year the first three members of her small community—Sisters Jodoka Villiger, Adela Eugster and Gertrude McDermott—departed for Fort Yates and the beginning of a completely new and quite unexpected apostolate. Later the sisters were to establish an interim motherhouse at Maria-Zell west of Redfield in southern Dakota. After that—again with the magnetism of Bishop Marty as an influencing force—they moved to Yankton.

But the story is getting ahead of itself . . .

Bishop Marty, torn by the defection of Sister Mary Paul, had other crosses to bear in early 1883. The *Bismarck Tribune* announced that a Catholic clergyman there had renounced

Romanism (he was also an alcoholic), and the *Elk Point Courier* publicized a fight between two Irish priests in that town. Then the citizens of Fargo signed a petition to stop the announced transfer of their pastor, and the *Fargo Argus* warned that "unless Bishop Marty revokes the edict, there will be trouble in the land." Any idea he might have had of devoting his energies more exclusively to the Indians was rudely shattered. He was caught up in the "Dakota boom" which in the brief eight years following his first trip from St. Meinrad had drastically altered the situation in the Territory.

In March of 1883 the territorial legislature passed a heatedly controversial measure, moving the capital from Yankton to Bismarck. Almost immediately the official residence of the Catholic bishop became a matter of great speculation. In April the *Pierre Signal* boasted:

> Bishop Marty has, we are reliably informed, definitely decided upon Pierre as his future abiding place, this being centrally located and very accessible. When a Catholic diocese is created for Dakota, it will be known as the diocese of Pierre.

Later the *Press and Dakotaian* reported, without a word of editorial comment, that the bishop "will have his home and ecclesiastical headquarters at Jamestown." Concerned as he may have been about the events and changes going on about him,

Like Martin Marty, Mother Gertrude Leupi was a Swiss Benedictine who answered the missionary call from America. She was instrumental in establishing St. Gertrude's Convent at Maryville, Missouri, after which—at the urging of Bishop Marty—she moved the community to Dakota Territory. (Sacred Heart Convent archives)

Marty was, as usual, too busy to give them more than cursory attention. Newspapers reported on a trip to Milwaukee where he was making arrangements for a seminary he planned to open in Yankton. In May of 1883 he had officiated at confirmation exercises at Wahpeton in northern Dakota where the church was badly damaged by lightning not long after he had left. From there he went to Standing Rock, to Pierre and then on to the Black Hills where he was warmly received and feted at Fort Meade, Deadwood and Rapid City. The *Deadwood Times* chronicled:

> Upon his first visit here three years ago, there was not even standing room in the church. Bishop Marty seems to command the affection of the members of his flock throughout the bishopric as well as the respect of all who know him.

The travel schedule continued unrelentingly: officiating, preaching, inspecting, teaching. In August he delivered a sermon at the ninth meeting of the American Cecelia Society in Cleveland. But there were moments of relaxation, too. In October the *Watertown Courier* announced:

> . . . Bishop Marty of Yankton held confirmation services in the church in Kranzburg Sunday last. In honor of the event some of the people had a jollification in the evening, and among other things done, six persons ate sixteen cans of raw oysters with their fingers, without using either knife, fork or spoon.

Chapter IX

Statehood and Changing Times

"Idleness is the enemy of the soul."
—The Rule of St. Benedict

At the beginning of 1884, Bishop Marty announced in his pastoral letter that he had nine students in his seminary, 82 churches in the vicariate and 45 priests to sustain them. Meanwhile, as the *Press and Dakotaian* of January 26 reported, he was pursuing still another venture:

> Bishop Marty is making preparations to occupy his residence on the west bluff, adjoining the convent of the Sacred Heart. He has in fair working order a plan to turn the convent building into an Indian school, under the auspices of the government . . . The bishop is a practical worker among the Sioux Indians and his idea is that schools for juvenile reds can be most successfully conducted nearer their homes than in the far eastern states [such as at Carlisle, Pennsylvania]. This is a suggestion which all who possess an understanding of the subject will endorse.

He had Benedictines from St. Meinrad and Conception working at Standing Rock, Crow Creek and Devils Lake. Secular priests were doing what they could on the Pine Ridge and Rosebud reservations until the bishop could find the means to establish permanent missions. The tiny parishes growing up along the proliferating railroad lines all demanded attention, too. In his new home, high on the bluff's edge overlooking the Missouri River, the 50-year-old prelate could not rest on his episcopal laurels; there was simply too much work to do!

At the new Indian school just a few yards from his house, the first contingent of boys seemed to be adapting to the program with the eagerness of youth of any race. By this time the bishop was well convinced that hopes for civilizing and Christianizing the Sioux rested mostly with the children. In full agreement with him on that score was James McLaughlin, the Catholic agent at Standing Rock, who in an official report advocated concentration on "the rising generation" because the conversion of adult Indians required "great patience and wonderful powers of perseverance." On July 15, the *Press and Dakotaian* noted:

> . . . Indian boys at the industrial school are picking up the rudiments of labor with surprising aptitude. They are in the hay field today and one of them finished and topped a stack with the skill of an old granger. They seem to like work and are ambitious to learn.

Father Willard brought additional boys to Yankton later in the summer, and the bishop himself took a group of Indian girls by train to Avoca, Minnesota, to enroll them in school there.

Politically, a new theme was being heard: statehood now! In southern Dakota an unauthorized constitutional convention in Sioux Falls, though unsuccessful, emphasized a divided territory. In northern Dakota there was strong sentiment for a single state with Bismarck as the capital. Whatever happened, of course, would certainly affect Bishop Marty's vicariate.

In November of 1884 he attended the Third Plenary Council of Baltimore; and because of his experience in the field, he was a dominant member of the committee considering the needs of Indians and negroes. An informal but disturbing topic of conversation at the assembly was the infamous political speech of Rev. Samuel D. Burchard—"Rum, Romanism and Rebellion"—which, with its anti-Catholic overtones, reputedly cost Republican James G. Blaine the presidency of the United States.

On April 1, 1885, Martin Marty, the mitered Benedictine from

Bishop Marty's residence (left), Sacred Heart Convent (center) and the academy building which served as an Indian school and later the original Sacred Heart Hospital were constructed on the prominence west of Yankton which became known as Mount Marty. (Sacred Heart Convent archives)

Switzerland, appeared in open court in Yankton, D. T., and officially became an American citizen. Five days later he left for New York where he boarded the *SS Servia* to make his first *ad limina* visit to Rome, the five-year obligation of bishops to travel "to the threshold" of St. Peter. Taking advantage of the ocean crossing, he drafted a lengthy report of his work among the Indians in Dakota. It had one major purpose: to help him recruit priests and raise money for the Sioux missions. Besides reporting to the pope, he intended to make as many speeches as possible in behalf of his cause, and he wanted a printed handout for his listeners and the press.

In his promotion message he wrote about Dakota Territory, the Indians themselves, the significance of the decreasing buffalo herds and the critical need for schools:

> "For the last eight years the 8,000 Indians of Pine Ridge, the 7,000 of the Rosebud and the 2,000 of the Crow Creek reservations have been begging me for schools, and I have had to put them off with promises of the future. If I cannot redeem these promises . . . then I shall have the sad duty to testify that the Dakotas have remained pagans not through any fault of their own but through ours."

Pope Leo XIII listened intently to the report from his vicar apostolic who represented him on the plains of mid-America. Much had been accomplished, he was told, but there were even greater opportunities if more priests and more money could be made available. As a gift from his prairie charges, the bishop presented the pontiff with an enormous buffalo robe, the leather side adorned by an Indian artist with various depictions of Siouian history, including the military triumph at Little Big Horn. He also had a gold medal of the Immaculate Conception blessed for James McLaughlin, the Catholic agent at Standing Rock. At the Vatican Marty also recommended that his widespread vicariate be cut in half to assure that the Indians and white settlers alike could be properly served. Before he left for Switzerland, he enjoyed a reunion with his brother, Father John Baptist Marty, chaplain of the pope's Swiss Guards.

What should have been a vacation for him developed into his usual high-geared work pattern. There were relaxing periods with his mother, of course, and with other relatives and the monks at Einsiedeln. But sandwiched between moments of leisure were speeches and sermons at Solothurn, Schwyz, Pfaffikon, Winterthur and wherever he might find interest in his work among the Sioux. Gratefully he accepted the returns from special collections: 1,200 francs here, 1,000 francs there. He traveled to England and Ireland; toured the Rhineland, including Würzburg and Munich on his itinerary; Vienna and Vorarlberg headed his list of stops in Austria. In September he was a featured speaker at an imposing Catholic congress (the *Katholiken-Versammlung*) at Muenster, Germany. He arrived back in the United States on October 10, just in time to attend the funeral of Cardinal John McCloskey, the first American-born clergyman to attain that ecclesiastical rank.

Meanwhile, there was intense activity of another kind going on in Yankton, D. T. It was finally becoming obvious to numerous citizens of the somewhat deflated ex-territorial capital that Bishop Marty's presence in their town had many advantages. On October 7, 1885, the editor of the *Press and Dakotaian* suggested:

> It is to the material interest of the people of Yankton to cooperate heartily with Bishop Marty in all his plans, and on his return from Rome next week to demonstrate to him that we appreciate the value of his presence as a resident . . .

The parishioners at Sacred Heart were already preparing for the bishop's homecoming. The sanctuary of the church was redecorated and a canopy was erected over the bishop's chair. The Sisters of St. Agnes were drilling their pupils for the celebration, as were the teachers at the Indian school. Businessmen were solicited for funds to buy fireworks for the event. Father Willard, as vicar general, invited the local militia to participate in the grand reception, but he was momentarily turned down on the

Looking northeasterly from the western bluffs where Bishop Marty lived, Yankton in the 1880s was still a busy little city but already falling behind Bismarck and Sioux Falls in its development. The territorial capital was moved to Bismarck in 1883, and six years later Sioux Falls lured Bishop Marty away. The latter, however, always expressed a fondness for the Mother City and indicated a desire to be buried there after his death—a wish unfulfilled. (Yankton County Historical Society)

basis that it would be "against regimental regulations."

But the newspaper editorial must have had a desired effect. Not only did Company E of the Dakota Militia turn out for the bishop's return on Thursday, October 22, but so did two companies of the fire department, the Edgerton Guard band, the Grand Army of the Republic, the mayor and city council, the boys of the Indian school, all the Sacred Heart students, many visiting clerics and a crowd of Yanktonians estimated at more than 2,000.

After his train pulled into the station, the bishop was taken first to Sacred Heart Church, his procathedral. Those who could get inside heard the choir sing a "Te Deum" and Julia Murphy, a student, recite a long poetic welcome, which included:

In spirit we were with you
'Mid St. Peter's lordly dome.
And 'mid tombs of sainted martyrs,
We trod each catacomb.

But now the days have vanished,
For us so drear and long,
And we greet again our bishop
With a hearty "welcome home!"

After the bishop responded briefly, the crowd poured from the church and mingled with the bigger throng outside. The procession reformed behind the boys of the Indian school bearing an American flag. Afoot and in carriages, the parade participants moved slowly to Main Street where banners of welcome spanned the intersections. Darkness had come, so candles were lit in business houses along the way, and the marchers carried torches as they cheered and enjoyed the music of the band. The queue made its way to the bishop's residence atop the western bluff where a gigantic reception was held. Hundreds of local citizens—many of them Protestants—met the bishop personally, ate the food prepared by Yankton's Catholic ladies, toured the Indian school, heard the Sioux youngsters sing (they had already been introduced to Gregorian chant) and watched the grand fireworks finale.

Possibly there were a few ulterior motives as hinted by the *Press and Dakotaian* story, but by and large, it was an honest, heartfelt welcome to a much beloved prelate.

✠ ✠ ✠

Before his traveling shoes hardly had time to cool down, he was off again, this time back to Washington, D. C. He had been

Louis Janousek, Yankton artist shown seated before a portrait of Abraham Lincoln Van Osdel, first photographed Bishop Marty (see opposite title page) and then painted him in a similar pose. After the photographing session, the bishop reputedly told Janousek that he didn't charge enough for his talent. (Janousek Family collection)

named to a special committee to promote the Catholic University of America, a prestigious assignment. But while he was in the area, he also had other business which needed attention.

He went to see Father Joseph Andreas Stephan, who had been appointed to head up the Catholic Indian Bureau following the death of Father Brouillet. Father Stephan—German-born son of an Irish mother and a Greek father—had turned to the priesthood after recovering from a loss of sight which forced him out of military school. He served as a Union Army chaplain during the Civil War and later had been appointed Indian agent at Standing Rock. Consequently, he had intimate knowledge of the situation in Dakota Territory, and he shared with Bishop Marty a sincere devotion to the cause of the Indian. Together they went to Philadelphia to see a young lady who—they had been informed—might be willing and able to help them in their work. The ensuing visit with Katharine Mary Drexel was to have a substantial long-range impact on the future of the Sioux Indian missions.

Kate Drexel was born on November 26, 1858, less than two years before young Father Martin Marty first came to America. She was the daughter of Francis A. Drexel and his first wife, Hannah Jane, who died shortly after Kate's birth. Drexel, like his father, was a prominent and wealthy

Philadelphia financier who died early in 1885, leaving Kate, her sister Elizabeth and step-sister Louise with an estate of more than fifteen million dollars.

Raised with all the advantages of great affluence, Kate Drexel never married and was inwardly burdened as she sought a worthwhile role for herself. In her earlier years she had come to know Father James O'Connor, pastor of St. Dominic Church in Holmesburg, Pennsylvania, near which the Drexels had a summer home. In time Father O'Connor became bishop of Omaha, the prelate who had jurisdiction over the Indian reservations west of the Missouri when Abbot Martin began his missionary services.

In 1887 Kate and Elizabeth were received in audience by Pope Leo XIII; and after she had directed to him an appeal for laborers among the Indians in America—an entreaty inspired in her by Bishop O'Connor, Bishop Marty and Father Stephan—he suggested that maybe she should become a missionary herself. In time that pontifical hint bore fruit, and on May 6, 1889, Katharine Drexel—at age 31—entered the novitiate of the Sisters of Mercy in Pittsburgh.

Two years later, when Sister Mary Katharine pronounced her vows, Bishop Marty was among the small assembly of guests in the chapel at Mercy Convent. Almost immediately Sister Katharine became Mother Katharine as she and 12 novices and postulants departed, as planned earlier, to establish a new order: the Sisters of the Blessed Sacrament for Indians and Colored People. In the ensuing years the contributions—in money and personal involvement—she was to make to the spiritual and temporal welfare of American Indians and blacks were immense and far-reaching. She died on March 2, 1955, in her 96th year.

When she was 27, however, she couldn't have envisioned the direction her life was to take as she went to greet Bishop Marty and Father Stephan, her then unknown callers . . .

Their mutual acquaintance with Bishop O'Connor established an immediate bond between the clergymen and Miss Drexel. They told her of the imperative need for schools to serve the Indians in Dakota Territory—and their message kindled a spark which was to develop into a burning flame in the months and years ahead. After so many other fruitless calls and contacts, the two missionaries had at last found a benefactor ready and eager to support their effort. As a result of the visit, Kate Drexel contributed $15,000 for a memorial building on the Rosebud reservation to be named the St. Francis Mission School in honor of her father's patron saint. It was erected on a 160-acre land grant Bishop Marty had received from the government for that purpose. Jesuits exiled from Germany arrived to take possession of the unfinished structure and begin a heritage of service at Rosebud and later at Pine Ridge. Holy Rosary Mission on the latter reservation also received a substantial Drexel donation.

Some might have called it a lucky break, but to Bishop Marty, the new association with Kate Drexel was Divine Providence at work. With periodic help from the Drexel fortune, at least some of the financial burden of the missions would be alleviated. On the Crow Creek reservation the bishop was able to move ahead, too, when another $15,000 came from Philadelphia for a school building, with a promise of $5,000 more for furnishings. Immaculate Conception Mission was established southeast of Pierre, with the postal address ultimately being named after Father Stephan, the Catholic Indian Bureau director. Father Pius Boehm, a Benedictine monk from St. Meinrad, was recruited to take charge of the new facility. Reminiscing some 45 years later, he recalled his arrival at the bleak outpost in January of 1887:

> "I was in the company of the late Bishop Marty. Coming to Highmore, we found that there was no room for us at the so-called hotel. Where the bishop slept, if he slept at all, I never learned, but I found a space behind a stove, where I slept the sleep of the just, in which I was soon joined by two stray dogs. The following day we arrived at Stephan where I have been ever since. The day after, our good Bishop left the mission and left me, not his mantle as in the story of the prophet of old, but his fur coat."

With Father Pius settled and on the job, Bishop Marty answered another summons. Louis Benziger, who had been one of Marty's students at Einsiedeln and was involved in the expansion of the family publishing business in America, asked his former teacher to write a biography of the bishop's friend and fellow religious from Einsiedeln, Archbishop John Martin Henni of Milwaukee. Despite his almost engulfing schedule, Marty agreed, but not before he had made arrangements for Father Vincent Wehrle (also from Einsiedeln and later first bishop of Bismarck) to take care of things for him in Dakota. The bishop's letter of instruction to the young priest—then recovering from "swamp fever" contracted in Arkansas—was a classic in succinctness:

> "My Vicar General [Father George Willard] has just died; as yet I have no one to replace him, so I am appointing you as my

Dr. Johann Martin Henni,

Erster Bischof und Erzbischof von Milwaukee.

Ein Lebensbild

aus der

Pionier-Zeit von Ohio und Wisconsin.

Von

Martin Marty, O. S. B.,

Apostolischer Vikar von Dakota und Bischof von Tiberias.

Zum

Andenken an das 50jährige Jubiläum des „Wahrheitsfreund".

Prämie zum 52. Jahrgang des „Wahrheitsfreund".

New-York, Cincinnati und Chicago.

Benziger Brothers,

Buchdrucker des heiligen Apostolischen Stuhles.

1888.

Despite his wearying schedule, Bishop Marty still found time to travel to Milwaukee to write the biography of his departed friend, Archbishop John Henni. The title page of the German-language volume is shown here. (Sacred Heart Convent library)

chancellor with the rights and duties of vicar general; on February 10, the Feast of Saint Scholastica, I am setting out for Milwaukee and there I shall write the biography of Archbishop Henni; I shall return at the beginning of Holy Week. You will open all letters addressed to me and answer them as well as you can. If you do not know what to do, write to me."

Sitting at Archbishop Henni's own desk, Marty—with his usual incessant drive—completed the 320-page biography of the dynamic Swiss-born prelate in the allotted time. The archbishop, who arrived in America the year Bishop Marty was born and who died in 1881, was a leader of German-speaking clergymen in the United States and founder of *Der Wahrheitsfreund*, an influential newspaper in Cincinnati which opposed slavery, prohibition and autocracy. Henni had been involved in the Irish-German controversy which plagued the Catholic Church in America intermittently for a long time.

Marty himself was periodically caught up in the ethnic feuding, although he gave evidence of attempting to pursue a middle road on that particular issue. However, while he was working in Milwaukee, a Bavarian German parishioner in Yankton stabbed an Irishman following an argument over a proposed separate German Catholic church. The wounded man survived and the idea of a second parish was dropped, but the incident illustrated the extent of the conflict between the two groups throughout the United States. It was more intense in the larger cities, of course, yet even in Dakota Territory it reached almost to the bishop's doorstep. Despite the intense feeling, there were no apparent public objections from Irish Catholics in Dakota when Bishop Marty named Father Otto Zardetti, another native of Switzerland, as his vicar general.

Meanwhile, rumors regarding the bishop's future residence continued to circulate. There was even one report that Marty was under consideration for appointment as archbishop of Detroit. On July 22, 1887, the *Press and Dakotaian* explained its view of church matters to community readers:

> Yankton's board of trade has taken steps to secure the permanent location of the heardquarters of Bishop Marty in this city. Catholic matters are assuming new shape in Dakota. A diocese is to be made of north Dakota and a diocese of south Dakota. This divi-

Otto Zardetti, an ambitious young Swiss priest, was Bishop Marty's second vicar general. In less than a decade Zardetti himself became bishop of St. Cloud and later was succeeded by Marty when Zardetti was transferred to Bucharest with the rank of archbishop. (Sacred Heart Convent archives)

> sion will occur at LaCrosse in August. Bishop Marty, who in the past has had the whole of Dakota as his diocese, has expressed his preference for the southern diocese and such assignment will be made . . . Yankton has long been the headquarters of Bishop Marty and does not want to part with its revered citizen. It will make a strong effort to retain so excellent a representative of this progressive church.

Six days later the newspaper published another story which told of a major change in the bishop's school program:

> On yesterday morning's Northwestern train, the Indian boys who have been students at Bishop Marty's Indian school in this city took passage for Crow Creek agency where commodious school buildings have recently been erected and where the boys will be nearer home. The buildings in this city which have been used for the school are now undergoing complete repairs, and in the fall a preparatory school for sisters of mercy who intend teaching in Dakota's missions will be opened there. Young lady boarders will also be accommodated, and as the course of study is to be under the personal jurisdiction of Bishop Marty, the school will be desirable as an educational institution. The sisters of the order of St. Benedict, who are now residing in Zell, Dakota, will have charge of the school, and it is presumed that the attendance will be very large.

Bishop Marty had appealed strongly to Mother Gertrude Leupi to move her convent from Maria-Zell to Yankton. Crowded conditions, lack of remunerative work for the sisters and high costs at the isolated location had been worrisome to her, and when the Indian school building at the former capital was vacated, she decided to take a closer look at the possibilities. Recovering from an energy-sapping illness herself, she traveled to Yankton where the bishop had invited her to recuperate. In one of her many letters back to Switzerland, she wrote:

> "There is a much healthier climate here than in Maria-Zell. Already I feel much better. The convent is located near a great river on somewhat elevated ground . . . The charm of the place is enhanced by a glorious view overlooking water, land and city. The Reverend Bishop has already paid thousands of dollars on the debt of the house, but there are more thousands to pay. If we accept the convent, we will incur the remaining debt . . . a burden of $15,000."

During her stay in Yankton, she occupied a room in the bishop's house, so from close proximity she was able to see the taxing scope of his labors. "The good bishop is overwhelmed with work," she wrote. "He told me he gets at least twenty letters on a given day, often five or six pages long." In the meantime, they discussed the merits of the proposed relocation, and finally the decision to move was made. Having the bishop so near at hand for counsel and spiritual care was an important factor of consideration. Mother Gertrude's admiration of Bishop Marty was revealed in her correspondence:

> "He is truly a holy bishop . . . He cares only for the salvation of others with a self-abnegation that is the wonder of all . . . We cannot thank God enough that we have found in this foreign land a father so solicitous and loyal as the bishop, who is at the same time a Benedictine . . ."

In September of 1887 Marty attended a meeting of the board of directors of the proposed Catholic University of America in Washington, D. C. Apparently he stopped off in Chicago some time during the trip because a news release from there indicated that an architect had been hired to draw up preliminary plans for extensive Catholic facilities in Yankton which would cost as much as $2,000,000. That same month Vicar General Zardetti bought

Benedictine sisters from Maryville, Missouri, moved first to Maria-Zell near Redfield in southern Dakota. In 1887 the community's motherhouse was transferred to Yankton following a strong appeal by Bishop Marty. (Sacred Heart Convent archives)

several lots in Yankton and it was speculated that a cathedral would be built to replace the old wooden house of worship. Later it was revealed that the priest had made the purchases with his own private funds as investments; they had nothing to do with the Catholic Church.

✠ ✠ ✠

On Bishop Marty's 54th birthday in 1888, a calamity of major proportions struck Dakota Territory. The particular day had dawned balmy and pleasant despite the midwinter date; children had trudged off to rural schools; farmers had driven to market or were away from home doing seasonal chores. Suddenly the mild southeast breezes brought a shower of rain, and then—without warning—the wind switched to the northwest, the temperatures plummeted and the rain turned to sleet and granular snow.

For more than a dozen hours the blizzard raged across the Territory. Men were trapped in the fields; livestock wandered aimlessly until they became stranded in drifts to freeze; but saddest of all, many youngsters were released by their teachers when the weather began to change and before they could get home, they were engulfed by the storm. In southern Dakota the gale gusted to more than 60 miles an hour and the mercury dropped to 20 degrees below zero or more.

Just as suddenly as it appeared, though, the "children's blizzard"—as it came to be known—passed out of the region. On Friday the 13th, survivors emerged from their places of safety to search for those who were not so lucky. When the gruesome figures were tallied, it was revealed that the January storm had left at least 112 dead in the southern half of the Territory. There was no way to determine how many others died later as a result of complications from exposure and freezing or how many amputations frontier doctors had to perform. At Immaculate Conception Mission one of the victims was 25-year-old Sister Wilhelmina Kaufmann, who was found kneeling in the deep snow after becoming lost in her attempt to get from the laundry to the main building. Bishop Marty, of course, was filled with compassion for those who experienced tragedy because of the storm and especially for the ill-housed Indians on the reservations.

Not long after the destructive ordeal, Marty fell and broke his arm. He was scheduled to give a lecture on St. Patrick's Day in Yankton, and although numerous advance tickets had been sold, he had to postpone his presentation on the life of the fabled Irish bishop. Two months later he was still in so much pain that he was unable to attend the cornerstone ceremonies for the Catholic University building in the nation's capital. On September 27, however, he was well enough to be the principal celebrant of the Mass at the consecration of John Ireland as archbishop of St. Paul. It marked the beginning of a new era of church administration in the Upper Midwest.

Late in 1888 it was announced that Bishop Marty was going to publish an official newspaper in Yankton. Early in the following year, however, it was publicly revealed that the *Yankton Herald* had won the bid for printing the first issue and for some reason or other had quit right in the middle of the job. Father Thomas F. Hopkins, then the bishop's secretary, published a notice of the default which said: "Under these annoying circumstances nothing can be done but to seek elsewhere such facilities for publication as seem to be unattainable in Yankton with due respect to business economy."

It is doubtful that the printing situation had any real effect on the ultimate decision to locate the diocesan see in Sioux Falls, but eight days later—on January 9, 1889—the *Press and Dakotaian* carried a one-sentence item almost hidden amid the daily local news:

> Bishop Marty is making preparations to leave Yankton and take up his residence elsewhere.

Early in February he moved out of his house on Mount Marty, and on the 22nd of the month President Grover Cleveland signed the omnibus bill which made the states of North and South Dakota, Idaho and Washington a reality. Later that same year, on November 2, President Benjamin Harrison signed the proclamations which officially created the two Dakotas as the 39th and 40th states of the Union. In doing so, the President shuffled the documents under a covering paper and signed them in such a way that no one would ever know what state preceded the other into the national federation.

While the statehood question was being settled, the reorganization of ecclesiastical jurisdictions was also proceeding. On September 29 Pope Leo XIII confirmed the establishment of five sees in the new episcopal province of St. Paul: Sioux Falls, South Dakota; Jamestown, North Dakota; St. Cloud, Duluth and Winona in Minnesota. As a result, Bishop Marty participated in a unique triple consecration ceremony two days after Christmas when Bishops James McGolrick of Duluth, John Shanley of

Jamestown and Joseph B. Cotter of Winona were elevated to their new dignity in the Cathedral of St. Paul. Following a gala dinner at the Ryan Hotel, numerous toasts were offered, among them one titled "Our Country" by Bishop Marty. The toasts undoubtedly were non-alcoholic because the clerics also included in their festive recognition the "Catholic Total Abstinence Union."

Throughout the momentous year of 1889, Bishop Marty continued to maintain his usual pace, involving himself in a multiplicity of details and divergent activities.

On February 26 he was appointed by President Harrison to serve on a special commission with Henry M. Rice of St. Paul, Minnesota, and Joseph B. Whiting of Janesville, Wisconsin, to negotiate with the Chippewa Indians of Minnesota for the cession of most of their reservation lands. Right or wrong, the bishop believed firmly that any action which, in effect, hastened tribal members down the road to civilization and ultimate Christianization could only lead to their benefit in the long run. His naivete and basic trust in the goodness of men seemingly did not permit him to question the sincerity of government or the motives of private citizens, and so he favored the relinquishment of Indian lands for a fair exchange. (Later he was to lodge a complaint that the Chippewas were being cheated in the sale of timber from their remaining reservation.)

In April of 1889 Mother Angela Arnet and four sisters from the Benedictine convent at Melchthal, Switzerland, took up temporary residence in a former wayside tavern in the Black Hills town of Sturgis. They had been invited to Dakota by Bishop Marty, who had made arrangements for them to stay at Yankton for a year until they learned sufficient English to conduct a school of their own. Shortly after the sisters arrived in Scooptown (the nickname was derived from the practice of "scooping" or "fleecing" the soldiers of nearby Fort Meade by local opportunists), construction was begun on an impressive sandstone structure which became St. Martin's Academy. Dynamic Father Peter Rosen, who served first as pastor at Deadwood, was the driving force behind the Sturgis academy, but when the project was stalled momentarily for fiscal reasons, the bishop intervened and the work was resumed. Although the great distance from Yankton—and later Sioux Falls—limited Marty's impact on the affairs of the Catholic Church in the Black Hills, he did influence and aid the development of early-day parishes throughout the region.

Despite his busy schedule—complicated by the decision to move his episcopal see to a new location—the bishop did not neglect the Indian missions. On June 17 he officiated at the ordination of Father Ambrose Mattingly at Stephan. He knew the appeal which the traditional rituals of the Church had for the Sioux, so he wanted them to be included in solemn liturgical rites whenever possible.

As he completed his tenth year as shepherd of a scattered and disparate flock, Bishop Marty faced still another notable change in his own life. His days as a roving black robe were coming to an end. The demands of a growing diocese in a brand new state would affect him more drastically than he might have imagined. At the same time, his move from Yankton was also keenly felt by the Benedictine sisters of Sacred Heart Convent, where Mother Gertrude Leupi wrote with obvious regret:

> "I expected 1889 to bring its cross, but . . . I can never express what the departure of our beloved Father Bishop cost us, so concerned was he always for our welfare."

Mother Gertrude herself, separated from the accessible counsel of the bishop and in failing health, resigned as superior. Later she returned to Switzerland where, in 1891, she established a third foundation—the Marienburg Convent at Wikon to recruit and educate Benedictine sisters for the missions in America. She was, like Mother Katharine Drexel, a providential angel sent at the appropriate time to assist Martin Marty in his work.

Chapter X

Burdens for the Bishop

"Sod houses, buggy beds, no privies, long wagon rides of eighty and ninety miles. Day after day of that life, and weeks of it at a stretch. No wonder stomach, liver, kidney, nerves, brain and everything in the human machinery went to pieces."

—Bishop John Shanley

Bishop Marty's move from Yankton to Sioux Falls in early February of 1889 was not without its controversial aspects. The competition for his presence had been keen, and the area newspapers reported the developments as they occurred. In Hurley the *Turner County Herald* editorialized:

> The citizens of Sioux Falls, with their usual enterprise, stole a march on Yankton. Taking advantage of the failure of Yankton parties to live up to their contract in the matter of the publication of the official organ of Bishop Marty, they subscribed $10,000 to erect the bishop a dwelling house in that city and this, along with other generous offers, has caused the bishop to move to the Queen city.

The *Sioux Falls Press*, flushed with the success of the promotion venture and envisioning even greater acquisitions for the city, boasted:

> ... Bishop Marty has commenced to remove his effects to this city from Yankton. Several loads of goods have already arrived and they have been put in the Seney house where the bishop will take up his residence ... It has been quite a struggle to get this prize, and all sorts of devices were resorted to to defeat the Queen city in her efforts.
>
> Two or three times the plum nearly slipped from the city's grasp, but a fresh hold was taken, and now the citizens have the satisfaction of knowing that for all time to come the Catholic headquarters of South Dakota will be in Sioux Falls ... now the head-

quarters for the following religious denominations: Catholic, Episcopal, Baptist and Norwegian. The city has an eye on the Methodist university in case Mitchell doesn't see fit again to gather it in.

Although Bishop Marty's diocese was limited to South Dakota, he was—because of his experience and personal interest—still in charge of the Indian missions within the old territorial bounds. Consequently, he, like others, was growing increasingly concerned about the restlessness of the Sioux.

In the 14 years following the Custer defeat in Montana and the opening of the Black Hills, the Dakota Indians were subjected to an erratic system of dole and control which was characterized by an enormous ignorance of the nature of the people themselves, their beliefs, their traditions, their nomadic lifestyle and even their capacity to comprehend what the white man called "civilization." Though the "peace policy" had some merit because of its attempt to take Indian affairs out of the hands of politicians and military officers, the emphasis was placed on Christianizing and industrializing the tribespeople with little thought apparently given to the depth or the values of the Indian culture itself.

When the policy changed and missionaries of various sects showed up on reservations previously allocated to specific denominations, it created further bewilderment among the Indians who—in addition to their other adjustments—had to cope with the revelation that Christianity came in different forms: Catholic "black robes," Episcopalian "white gowns" and Congregational and Presbyterian "short coats." Though the

Sioux Falls provided Bishop Marty with an impressive stone residence when he moved from Yankton in 1889. The house later was given to the Presentation Sisters who utilized it as part of the McKennan Hospital School of Nursing before it was razed in the early 1970s. (Sacred Heart Convent archives)

various church representatives, by and large, were sincere in their efforts to "help" their wards on the reservations, they exhibited varying degrees of intelligence, ability, zeal and understanding—and, in fact, competed for the souls of the Sioux who were referred to quite generally as "heathens," "pagans" and "savages." Martin Marty himself was not totally free of shortcomings in this regard, though his pietistic paternalism seemed to stem more from over-zealous concern for the spiritual and temporal welfare of the Indians than merely for a high boxscore of conversions. Like the vast majority of whites on the frontier, he, too, gave little consideration to what the tribespeople really thought or believed—but his good intentions could not be faulted in the slightest.

On February 10, 1890, President Harrison signed the proclamation which wiped out the Great Sioux Reserve. Earlier the Treaty of 1889 had defined boundaries of the eight reservations left to the Dakota Indians. As a tidal wave of land-seekers moved across the Missouri River onto the ceded territory, the smoldering resentment of the tribes was rekindled. Angry and frustrated, the Sioux understandably were receptive to any course which might bring back the old ways. In addition to everything else, a drouth had descended upon the area, wiping out the hayfields and tiny gardens of those Indians who were trying to adjust to a new lifestyle—with no agricultural experience and on land which was woefully poor for farming purposes.

It was no wonder that the Dakotas listened intently when they heard of a new Indian Messiah who was preaching a message of deliverance near Pyramid Lake, Nevada. Wovoka, a Paiute dreamer known less glamorously as Jack Wilson, claimed to have had a revelation which—while stressing mostly the Christian virtues of hope and love—was tailored to the emotional needs of the tribes at that particular time. If the Indian people wore "ghost shirts" and participated in the Ghost Dance, Wovoka said, the buffalo would return, the white men would disappear, their relatives would rise from the dead, bullets would not penetrate their flimsy calico vests and all their lost land would be restored.

The Ghost Dance and a garbled form of Wovoka's philosophy reached the Sioux just when they needed it most; supposedly the phenomenon was to occur "when the grass began to grow in the spring" of 1891. Since dancing was a cherished part of Dakota religious expression (a custom white men long had difficulty understanding), many Indians welcomed the new cult and its supernatural features. It filled a void, and it had nothing to do with an armed uprising; after all, the message promised that all they had to do was wait, dance and "do right" and their burdens would be lifted from them.

For missionaries—including Bishop Marty—all of this was difficult to comprehend. It was pagan in nature and detrimental to the progress they thought they had made. The military commanders (some of them still eager for vengeance) considered the Ghost Dance a threat, as did the homesteaders who were always wary of the Sioux.

And there was an additional element in the historical drama!

Sitting Bull, the controversial and colorful Hunkpapa with whom Marty had established more than a casual relationship, had been returned from Fort Randall to the Grand River country where he was living in a log cabin when the so-called Messiah Craze developed. It was rumored that he was somehow involved in the new religious fervor and would use it to foment a revolt. Consequently, to head off such an eventuality, the commander at Fort Yates was ordered to arrest him before greater trouble erupted.

In the early dawn of December 15, 1890, a detachment of 43 Indian policeman headed by Lieutenant Bull Head arrived at Sitting Bull's cabin. They were supported by a detail of cavalry troopers who halted outside the camp to avoid inciting an unnecessary conflict. A scuffle followed Bull Head's confrontation with the aging medicine man, and in the exchange of gunfire which followed, Sitting Bull and Bull Head were both mortally wounded, along with six members of the Indian police unit and an unknown number of resisting warriors.

Two weeks later—at Wounded Knee Creek, 17 miles northeast of the Pine Ridge Agency headquarters—one of the most infamous incidents in American history occurred. A small band of Minneconjous under Chief Big Foot had been intercepted by the reconstituted Seventh Cavalry, Custer's old regiment which still bore the stigma of the Little Big Horn defeat. The Indians had been proceeding southward through the Badlands, either to turn themselves in at Pine Ridge (as the Sioux claimed later) or to join the rapidly increasing band of Ghost Dancers (as the army believed). During the disarming, a shot was fired, and the senseless massacre began. When it was over, between 200 and 300 Indians—including infants—were dead, and the number of those who perished in the snow and cold which followed the terrible onslaught has never been accurately determined.

The Wounded Knee Massacre—which was to become an Alamo for the Sioux—left a lingering scar on white-Indian relationships which would persist for generations. At the same time the date became an historical dividing line: the Great Sioux Nation had been humbled, Custer had been ingloriously avenged, and the promise of the Ghost Dance was forever gone.

In a way the carnage at Pine Ridge marked a dividing line in the life of Martin Marty, too. Although he was not directly involved, he had sent a telegram to Holy Rosary Mission, instructing Father John Jutz and the sisters there to abandon the installation if danger became imminent. Fortunately, neither they nor the facilities were harmed, and the mission played an important role in the aftermath as a refuge for women and children.

The frontier missionary phase of Bishop Marty's personal career, if not over, was certainly altered. All of a sudden diocesan concerns began to engulf him; and although he lost none of his ardor for service to the Indian people, he was faced more and more with the demands of growing towns and parishes.

✠ ✠ ✠

Throughout his lifetime, Martin Marty was bedeviled by controversy, and much of it he created either directly or indirectly himself. In many ways he remained always a humble, prayerful monk; but at the same time—in his dealings with other people, especially priests and sisters—he could be dominant and benevolently dictatorial. He never quite lost his youthful traits of caustic retort and quick judgment, although there is evidence, in what he wrote and said, that he tried to curb the failing. "Sometimes the wild horse runs away with me" is the way he himself described his personal shortcoming.

"Our bishop is *rasch,*" one elderly Sister supposedly said of him. And in German or English, the word was at various times appropriately descriptive. Sharp of mind, almost to the point of brilliance, he seemed to lack patience with mental laggards among his fellow religious. Former monastic students have described him as a demanding, almost ruthless teacher; but with Indians, struggling to learn, he could exhibit warmth and understanding.

The correspondence of Mother Gertrude Leupi reveals the depth of his concern for the needs of the sisters—especially the Swiss—who joined him in America's hinterland. On one occasion, he personally conducted English lessons for a homesick young nun, easing her over her emotional crisis until she could adjust to her new setting. Sometimes he got more involved than he should have been, even to the point of shopping for the convent. It was not unusual, one report states, to see Bishop Marty returning up the hill from Yankton with new shoes for the sisters under his arm.

On more than one occasion he interfered in the religious practices of sisters under his authority, creating dissension as he had when he dogmatically altered the Divine Office traditions of the Benedictine monks at St. Meinrad. But he also tried to alleviate contention, too, as he did when he invited the several rebellious Sisters of Mercy from Omaha to Yankton in the late 1870s and promptly inherited the fruits of their internal bickering. Letters he exchanged with Bishop O'Connor expressed a lack of sympathy for the dilemma which the sisters ultimately fashioned for themselves, not the least of which was Sister Mary Paul's personal defection. However, an indication that Marty was not vindictive was revealed in the *Yankton Press and Dakotaian* on January 24, 1890, when it was announced that Dr. V. Sebiakin-Ross had been reappointed convent physician. The story concluded:

> . . . His convent appointment was made by Bishop Marty. It is a position he once held and forfeited by inducing one of the sisters to become Mrs. Sebiakin-Ross. That he is restored to favor indicates a forgiving spirit in the Catholic church.

In her definitive history of Sacred Heart Convent, *Under the Shadow of His Wings,* Sister Claudia Duratschek described how the bishop, even though he had moved to Sioux Falls, still maintained intense personal interest in the sisters he had left behind:

> . . . Sister Xavier [Fischlin, appointed acting superior] could always turn to Bishop Marty for counsel and guidance. Indeed, after Mother Gertrude's return to Switzerland his concern for the Yankton community doubled. He assumed practically the whole responsibility for its welfare. Was not he the one who had induced the sisters to brave the hazards of pioneer conditions, in stark poverty and deadening isolation, to come to his aid in the apostolate on the Dakota frontier? This solicitude for the sisters' spiritual and temporal welfare often caused him to become deeply involved in their community affairs. An outsider might have interpreted this relationship as meddling. That it was considered in this light at times can be gathered from a letter Sister Xavier wrote Mother Gertrude less than a month after the latter's departure. She reported that the bishop was acting as though he were the superior of the convent. He had presumed to reprimand an offending sister. He had even taken upon himself to make several changes in mission assignments. Yet, no one ever questioned the fact that his conduct was inspired only by his zeal for God's service, which seemed to consume him; many did, however, question the wisdom of some

measures. It must be stated to his credit that whenever he acted rashly, he did not neglect to admit his error of judgment and to do his utmost to rectify his mistake.

In 1892 Sister Xavier was officially elected superior of the Yankton convent. However, a group of sisters continued their loyalty to Mother Gertrude despite her absence and, as a result, created problems within the community. The bishop—without much investigation—sided with the dissenters, removed Mother Xavier precipitously, sent her "in exile" to the Sturgis convent, and appointed Sister Mathilda Cattani to succeed her. Later, when he learned the facts of the case, he recalled Sister Xavier and sent her as superior to the Fort Yates mission. (In 1904 she was again elected prioress of Sacred Heart Convent and served for almost 20 years in that role.)

In the meantime, Bishop Marty created still new problems for the Yankton sisters by sending them an Italian priest and two women members of the Third Order of St. Francis who had tried unsuccessfully to establish an orphanage in Sioux Falls. With six homeless girls, ranging in age from 9 to 12, they were virtually destitute and desperately in need of help. Magnanimously, the bishop shipped them off to his former home, confident that he was providing the sisters with a chaplain (to replace one he had removed) and the diocese with a much needed orphanage. The arrangement was never satisfactory, however, and soon the Franciscans and their young charges left "for parts unknown." Having committed the Benedictine sisters to a new but relatively brief mission, the bishop continued to send orphans to them for several years, after agreeing to pay eight dollars a month per child for their keep.

Though his various difficulties involving sisters were aggravating and provoked more than an occasional venial sin of anger, they were—for the most part—internal and out of the public eye. The same was not true of his confrontations with certain strong-willed and contentious priests in the diocese.

It must be remembered, of course, that South Dakota was a new state and that the region itself had been unsettled frontier slightly more than thirty years earlier. It took individuals of unique strength, tenacity and sometimes eccentricity to volunteer for service on the remote prairies. Before and after he became a bishop, Marty welcomed all the help he could get; and in the process he accepted—along with the good priests—a small contingent of malcontents, alcoholics and assorted troublemakers which eastern prelates were happy to send him. This willingness to harbor men of questionable stability could only lead to delayed repercussions—some minor, some intense.

Marty had been sent to America as a young man in 1860 to counter the head-strong actions of Father Ulrich Christen at St. Meinrad. From that time on he had experienced numerous personality clashes which—because priests and bishops are human, too—marred the otherwise outstanding religious achievements on the mid-American frontier. Before he left Yankton he had been caught up in a prolonged and distasteful controversy involving Abbot Alexius Edelbrock of St. John's Abbey in Minnesota, who was charged with having greater concern for material than for spiritual development. As he had done in the case of Mother Xavier, Bishop Marty accepted the stories of the dissidents—Fathers Othmar Erren and Ambrose Lethert—assigning Father Ambrose to mission work in northern Dakota and granting priestly faculties to Father Othmar, who had been suspended by Abbot Alexius for writing inflammatory articles under the pseudonym, "Aurora Borealis." The Dakota bishop backed Father Othmar's appeal all the way to Rome, writing letters of recommendation and introducing him to his own brother, Monsignor John Marty, with instructions to assist the complaining monk in his cause.

As it turned out, Bishop Marty's stance alienated himself from many Benedictine abbots and monks. Even his own brother reported that Father Othmar had left a poor impression in Rome; and at Einsiedeln—before his return to America—he was not even permitted to say Mass. Whether it was a case of gullibility, compassion or honest conviction, Marty reaped only bitter fruit from the episode and undoubtedly cost himself some measure of sympathy when he—like Abbot Alexius—became the victim of priestly rebellion a few years later. When Father Othmar was warned that he might not be welcomed back to St. John's, he reputedly said: "Two cents and a few lines to Bp. Marty will get me another place . . ."

Among the priests who served in Dakota Territory was Father Robert W. Haire, who came west with a colonizing party from Flint, Michigan, in 1880. Flamboyant, outspoken and given to populist philosophies, Father Haire filed on a claim near Columbia in Brown County and was instrumental in the creation of parishes in Groton, Redfield, Huron, Aberdeen and other communities in the region. Working closely in concert with Bishop Marty at first, Father Haire in 1887 became editor of the *Dakota Catholic American*, the first Catholic newspaper in the Territory. Published in Aberdeen, the periodical soon began to reflect the editor's personal views on labor reform, temperance, women's suffrage and other issues often more political than religious.

Bishop Marty quickly became concerned about the position of the Church with such an aggressive spokesman, and a rift soon developed. Within a year Father Haire announced his resignation as editor, and shortly thereafter began to espouse his causes in the columns of the Knights of Labor publication. In his writings he referred to the bishop as "that old rascal in Sioux Falls" and other less-than-complimentary phrases, and in time he became so reckless and abusive that he was forced to make a decision between the priesthood and politics. In 1889 he chose the latter, being one of the founders of the South Dakota Populist Party and championing the inclusion of the initiative and referendum processes in the state constitution. Because of his access to the public press—especially through the *Aberdeen Star*—he remained a nagging thorn for Bishop Marty. The *Sioux Falls Press*, angered because of several articles about the bishop, editorially chastised the *Star* for permitting "Father" Haire "to make its columns a sewer for his gall." (In 1901 Haire was restored to full practice of the priesthood.)

Meanwhile, Marty suddenly found himself publicly under attack from two disgruntled priests, demanding his removal and castigating him for ineffective and "ruinous" management of the

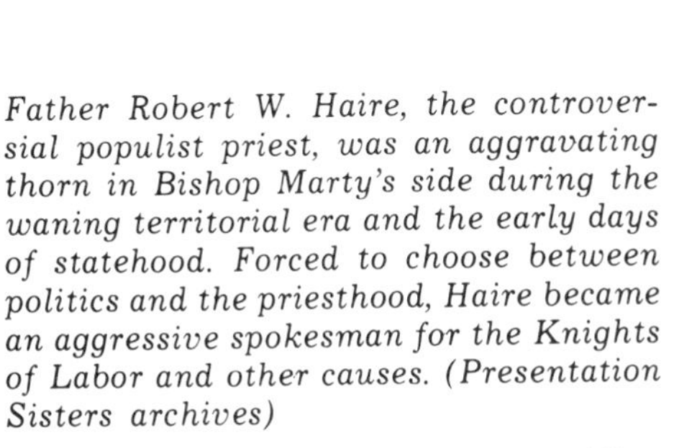

Father Robert W. Haire, the controversial populist priest, was an aggravating thorn in Bishop Marty's side during the waning territorial era and the early days of statehood. Forced to choose between politics and the priesthood, Haire became an aggressive spokesman for the Knights of Labor and other causes. (Presentation Sisters archives)

diocese. The ill-defined charges were widely printed in the press and relayed to Rome. Later, when they were referred back to Archbishop John Ireland in St. Paul, Father J. C. Ahern, one of the complainants who had been suspended by Marty, charged further that the case was being purposely delayed by the archbishop. (Not long afterward, Father Ahern was convicted of assaulting one of his Flandreau parishioners with a rock.)

Bishop Marty, who was beginning to show signs of physical and emotional exhaustion, did not lack for support. Loyal priests of the diocese issued a statement which was published on August 30, 1893:

> During the past couple of months there has appeared in newspapers throughout the country articles bearing on the character of Bishop Marty, and statements made derogatory to the bishop's character. This week a synod of the Catholic priests of this diocese has been in session at the residence of Bishop Marty, which has been presided over by Father Joseph A. Stephan, vicar general. The following resolutions were passed unanimously yesterday by the clergy of this diocese, with exception of the two aggrieved parties, and they show the respect and esteem in which Bishop Marty is held despite the false and malicious accusations uttered against him:
>
> "In view of the manner our beloved bishop has been villified in the public press by certain incorrigible and malicious priests now known to the prelate of Sioux Falls and his clergy; be it
>
> "Resolved. That we, the priests of Sioux Falls diocese in synod convened, feel it our bounden duty to give public expression of our confidence in the estimable ordinary of this diocese. The saintliness of his character, his rare administrative ability, his absolute freedom from national and partial prejudice, his noble example of every Christian virtue, are known and felt by the clerics and lay people of South Dakota. Further, be it
>
> "Resolved. That all articles defamatory to the character of Bishop Marty and his priests are vile calumnies and the originators thereof are infamous liars and passionate creatures of ecclesiastical disappointment.
>
> "Since patience has its limits and as a philosopher said, '*Est modus in rebus, sunt certi denique finis quos ultra citraque nequit cons'stere rectum,*' be it finally resolved that we the priests of Sioux Falls diocese have demanded of our diocesan authority that the perpetrators be legally dealt with according to their deserts in the ecclesiastical courts."

The old, belabored issue of favoritism for German-speaking priests over the Irish was raised again, but apparently not all the Sons of Erin felt ill-treated. Among the signatories of the resolution were Fathers Sheehan, Flynn, Flanigan, Shea, Collins, Hogan, McNally, Nolan, Kennedy and Kelly.

Dedicated and devoted as he was, Bishop Marty couldn't help but be affected by the strange turn of events which had suddenly altered his life. In the aftermath of Wounded Knee, the Indian mission program had to be reassessed. Statehood, the creation of a South Dakota diocese and the move from Yankton to Sioux Falls were all factors of change for him.

No longer was it possible to concentrate on the needs of the Sioux. He became involved in the promotion of total abstinence societies when it became apparent that the state's prohibition law not only failed to curb the consumption of alcohol but caused temperance groups to reduce their vigilance. This, of course, was a stance not universally popular with either his German or his Irish church members. At the same time it was widely publicized that South Dakota's embryonic laws offered loopholes for easy dissolution of marriage. As a result, Sioux Falls for a brief period became known as the "divorce capital of the nation," with Yankton challenging the Queen City for that dubious honor. For Bishop Marty and other clerics this attack on a sacred institution was an onerous situation demanding counter measures to amend the law. In this he became an ally of his former missionary competitor, Episcopalian Bishop Hare. In his own cathedral parish—St. Michael's of Sioux Falls—he was understandably disturbed by a controversy which raged between the pastor, Father W. V. Nolan, and the sisters who had taught in the school. The case was carried all the way to Rome and ended ultimately with the priest being "advised" to apologize publicly—which he did, with reservations!

On top of everything else, the Panic of 1893 brought economic burdens to the diocese which had not been expected when Sioux Falls had so generously promised to do wonderful things for the bishop if he would move from Yankton. When the local citizens could not or would not meet their obligations, the property had to be mortgaged; and in a letter to a friend at Einsiedeln, Marty wrote: "My life is insured for $10,000, so if I should die, my debts can at least be paid."

To make matters worse, the drouth in the summer of 1894 matched or exceeded any of the previous dry spells since the earliest territorial days, and farmers joined businessmen in failure. Priests of the diocese were equally hard-pressed, and one of them—Father D. F. Desmond—later recalled: "The good saintly bishop gave us all the comfort he could at $600 a year. He meant well and showed a good example in his own manner of living."

As if he didn't have enough distractions and detractors, Bishop Marty also got embroiled in a political hassle preceding the general election of 1894. In a letter to some—not all—of the priests of the diocese, he asked them to "Please use your influence . . . to the end that Richard F. Pettigrew may be returned to the senate." Somehow the letter was made public, and a minor uproar developed, with Catholic Democrats joining Protestants and anti-Catholics in remonstrating against the bishop. Again he was the subject of both editorial attack and support. The *Sioux Falls Press* of November 3, 1894, described the extent to which the tempest-in-a-teapot had been ballooned:

> . . . Another anonymous circular . . . has been printed in Scandinavian and scattered over the state, a copy of which, with its translation, is in possession of *The Press*. The heading of this circular is a sufficient indication of its contents: "A Terrible Discovery! A Catholic Conspiracy!"
>
> The purpose of this is of course to delude the people into the idea that by reason of Bishop Marty's personal indorsement of Senator Pettigrew's candidacy for re-election, "a vote for Pettigrew's republican legislative candidates is a vote for Catholics and for Catholic supremacy in America." That is what the circular says. But it is scarcely likely that any considerable portion of the Scandinavian voters, whom it is intended to gull, can be fooled thereby.
>
> A little singular—isn't it?—that the opposition should regard the election of Senator Pettigrew as a step toward "Catholic Supremacy," when he is not a Catholic, while the same opposition is supporting Stephen Donahoe for the legislature, who is a Catholic. There are very few who will urge objection against Mr. Donahoe on account of his being a Catholic, but those who are alarmed by Bishop Marty's letter have certainly less reason for raising objection against Senator Pettigrew who is not identified with the church.

Outwardly the bishop seemed to ride with the punches, but more and more there was concern about the condition of his health. A stomach ailment brought on by extended existence on a poor diet and lengthy fasting added to his physical suffering. Though his travel schedule in the early 1890s continued with little curtailment, there was some thought that by his 60th birthday, he might already be pushing himself "on borrowed time." In the hierarchy of the Church, where Marty's over-burdening situation had been perceived, action was already underway to ease the pressures upon him in hopes that his life and his good works might be prolonged.

✠ ✠ ✠

Just before Christmas of 1894 the bishop was in Aberdeen where he participated in the selection of a successor to the late Mother Aloysius Chriswell of the Presentation convent. On that occasion the *Aberdeen News* reported that "His appearance indicates that his health has very materially improved, and acquaintances take pleasure in congratulating him thereon." A week later, on December 31, the *St. Paul Pioneer Press* announced:

> Archbishop Ireland received a message yesterday to the effect that Bishop Marty, now of the bishopric of Sioux Falls, S. D., has

St. Michael's Church in Sioux Falls became Bishop Marty's second procathedral following his move from Yankton. It was later demolished to make room for the new St. Joseph's Cathedral dedicated in 1919. (St. Joseph's Cathedral Parish archives)

been transferred by the pope to the bishopric of St. Cloud, which was made vacant by the transferral of Bishop Zardetti to Bucharest.

> Bishop Marty is one of the best known bishops in the United States. He was made a bishop in 1880, and was moved to Sioux Falls in 1889, when the bishopric was established in that place. Under his jurisdiction now are about seventy or eighty churches. His work in South Dakota has been much among the Indians, and in that work he has become one of the most influential of men. He has had charge of the establishment of a number of Indian missions, and is beloved by the people . . . as well as considered by the pope a most efficient worker and an authority on Indian church affairs.

Even before the official news had been received, there was speculation about the move and a possible successor. Concurrently, there was also divided opinion concerning the reasons for the episcopal shift. The *Yankton Press and Dakotaian* explained:

> It is maintained at the Sioux Falls end of the discussion that Bishop Marty is taken away from South Dakota because of trouble he has encountered in the administration of the affairs of the church. Father [Edward] Jones, of Yankton, says this is wholly incorrect. He says the bishop is in poor health and is physically unable to keep up his travels over the diocese as has been his habit . . . The motive in the change is to give a faithful servant a diocese which can be managed with less bodily exertion. This is probably the correct explanation.

With mixed emotions—and Benedictine obedience—the bishop accepted the transfer to succeed his former vicar general at St. Cloud, a small central Minnesota city named for St. Clodoald, patron of French nail-makers. On February 2, 1895, a farewell party was held for him at his residence in Sioux Falls, complete with a "very elaborate literary and musical programme" by the pupils of St. Rose Academy. A week later he boarded a Great Northern train for the trip to his new and final place of service. At St. Cloud he was greeted by "all the Catholic societies in the city, headed by the union band and the priests of the diocese." A procession of some 1,500 parishioners and church dignitaries escorted him to the procathedral where Archbishop Ireland officially installed him.

Bishop Marty was not, as some folks thought, merely being "put out to pasture."

Chapter XI

The Final Mile, the Last Amen

"A quiet conscience sleeps in thunder."
—Thomas Fuller

Bishop Marty's personality, character and physical stoicism are revealed best in actual incidents recorded in the reminiscences of those who knew him. Near Stump Lake in Nelson County, northern Dakota, for instance, Ursuline sisters filed on two homestead claims in 1884, and in their tar-paper shanty they taught catechism to the children of settlers in the vicinity. In time they had 17 youngsters prepared for confirmation but with very little hope that the bishop in far-away Yankton would ever be near enough to their prairie abode some sixty miles west of Grand Forks so that the sacrament could be administered.

In a letter to him they offered to bring the children to a rendezvous anywhere along the railroad tracks "if His Excellency could manage to stop the train." To their great delight, they received a reply that the bishop would not only stop the train, he would come to their shanty nine miles south of the line on the fourth of July!

Their 20x20-foot rough-board "convent" was somehow divided into three sections, the end with the wallpaper being assigned as "the bishop's room." In it was an altar decorated with wild flowers drenched by leaks in the roof. A classroom was located in the middle compartment, with a kitchen—crammed almost beyond description—at the other end. Strategically placed pots and pans caught the rainwater dripping through the cracks above.

According to the sisters' recollections, the bishop arrived, removed his sodden coat, sat down on a drygoods box with a shawl over his shoulders, put his feet in the oven, and began to instruct the children. Heavy rains kept nine of the 17 confirmands away, but the bishop, unperturbed by the size of his class or his own personal discomfort, officiated at the holy rite with as much devotion as he would have shown in a magnificent cathedral.

The memoirs of other missionaries invariably included references to Bishop Marty's calm, uncomplaining acceptance of privation and suffering as he roamed the frontier. Father Bernard Strassmaier, who himself served for 54 years on the Standing Rock Reservation, recalled one particular journey:

> "On July 5, 1892, in company with several missionaries (of whom one was the writer), Bishop Marty started from Cheyenne Agency on a trip to the agency at Standing Rock. The route led by way of Bullhead, S. D., to Fort Yates, N. D. The distance was about 100 miles. The first night's rest was on the ground in a poorly constructed tent. Next morning a journey of twenty miles was made without breakfast. After crossing the dangerous Moreau River and partaking a frugal meal, the remainder of the journey was made amidst a storm of thunder and rain.
>
> "In the evening, after fording the Grand River, the tent was pitched on the wet ground and a meager supper gave sustenance to the fatigued body . . . a restless night and much worry followed, as we were still fifteen miles from Bullhead where the new church of St. Aloysius was to be dedicated. Though the roads were in a bad condition, His Lordship determined to go on fasting for the balance of the journey. In consequence of a fall from the lumber wagon in which he was poorly seated, the bishop had the misfortune to dislocate his ankle.
>
> "Finally we arrived at Bullhead, near noon, and at once made preparation for the celebration of the Mass. By this time the pain from the injured ankle was intense, and it was with great difficulty that the bishop was able to complete the Holy Sacrifice. Then it was found that the bishop could not walk nor stand because of his injured foot. After partaking of a light breakfast, the lumber wagon was fitted out as a bed for the bishop. In this pitiable condition, after a journey of forty miles, St. Benedict's Mission was finally reached . . . The injured foot had now become so badly swollen that the journey to Fort Yates had to be postponed.
>
> "Throughout this agonizing ordeal, so hard on his weakened constitution, the bishop never uttered a word of complaint. Like a hero, patiently he bore the pain in the spirit of submission to God's holy will . . ."

Father Chrysostom Foffa, in later years, related how Marty, who was severe with himself, also expected others to accept a share of suffering. On an occasion when the bishop visited Father Chrysostom in his tent on the open prairie, he noted that there was a mosquito netting over the latter's cot. Commenting that he considered such a protective device a luxury ill-becoming a monk, he refused one for himself. The next morning when Marty arose, his face was a mass of insect bites. With an understanding smile, he agreed with his fellow Benedictine that "under some circumstances, a mosquito net is not a *luxus*!"

These, of course, were typical examples of Bishop Marty's willingness to go wherever his people needed him, under whatever conditions were involved. The thousands of miles he traveled by the limited means of the period consumed a large portion of his working hours, but with him the time was never wasted. Coated with train dust or soot from the belching stacks of early-day locomotives and paddlewheel steamers, he meditated, wrote and prayed as the tedious miles passed beneath rail-bound Pullmans,

Bishop Marty utilized every available means of transportation in his seemingly endless travels. He rode the Dakota Southern Rail Road in and out of Yankton and journeyed up and down the Missouri on the numerous river steamers which delivered annuity goods to the various reservation pickup points. (Yankton County Historical Society)

Sioux Falls, South Dakota,
June 1, 1894.

Received of Benedictine Convent of the Sacred Heart of Yankton, South Dakota, on debt of Twenty-Five Thousand Dollars, (per Warranty-deed, dated Feb. 8, 1889, and filed for Record, February 11, 1889, at 12 o'clock, in Book 42, on Page 509, Yankton County) by and between Rt. Rev. Bishop, Martin Marty, Yankton Dakota, and Benedictine Convent of the Sacred Heart, Yankton, Dakota, the sum of Thirteen Thousand Dollars ($13,000) in partial Payments in Cash with interest in full to date, and Six Thousand Dollars by my donation to said Benedictine Convent of the Sacred Heart, in total the sum of Nineteen Thousand Dollars ($19,000).

+ Martin Marty O.S.B.
Bp. of Sioux Falls.

Bishop Marty's close involvement with the sisters of Sacred Heart Convent in Yankton is revealed in this receipt, which includes a personal contribution. (Sacred Heart Convent archives)

vertebrae-wrenching stagecoaches, plodding wagons and sandbar-skimming riverboats. His writing board was his almost constant companion, and he maintained his extensive correspondence beside campfires, in rustic reservation quarters or wherever there was time to apply pen to paper in the precise, diminutive style which characterized his writing.

Multi-talented as he was, he wrote, preached and played the organ with a simplicity which may have belied his genius. When Marty delivered the sermon at the dedication of St. Agnes Church in Vermillion on August 15, 1890, a reporter for the *Dakota Republican* offered the following appraisal:

We found much to admire in his style of diction, powers of analysis and straightforward earnestness. He is a profound scholar, and yet all his sentences were so simply constructed that a child could easily comprehend them. In personal appearance and manner he is the personification of benevolence, kindliness, sincerity and courtesy. Dignified, not austere; scholarly, not cynical: a father and a friend.

Not given to banter or frivolous commentary, he did show occasional glimpses of a restrained and sometimes biting sense of humor. On one occasion when he was served a dessert at one of the missions and told it was good for the singing voice, his reply was totally unexpected. Earlier young nuns had failed miserably at singing an unfamiliar Mass for the Dead to Marty's accompaniment on the organ. Consequently, the bishop suggested that it was too bad the sweetmeats had not been "served to the sisters this morning *before* the Requiem."

At another time when a sister was assigned to sit next to him at table and she protested her unworthiness of the place of honor, he smilingly instructed her that while humility was a worthy virtue, it is even "more perfect to do as we are told."

While he never disavowed his Swiss heritage, he adjusted readily to his adopted land and gave no evidence of a desire to return ultimately to Einsiedeln as others had done. However, that there existed a nostalgic yearning for the "Old Country" on occasion might be concluded from a news story which appeared in the *Sioux Falls Press* on November 24, 1893:

Bishop Marty received yesterday from Cincinnati, O., through the United States Express company, a St. Bernard dog that is the largest animal of its kind in the city. The dog came in a crate which, with the animal, weighed 225 pounds. It was estimated that the crate weighed fifty, so it would leave 175 pounds of dog . . . The dog measures about seven feet from the tip of its nose to the tip of its tail and it acted as if it was as fierce as it looked.

Unfortunately, though the pet may have stirred Alpine memories, it apparently brought additional problems which the bishop certainly didn't need at the time. Several months later, the *Press* carried the following advertisement:

For Sale Cheap

A full-blooded St. Bernard with registered pedigree; would not sell only having such a large dog, people do not like to call on business. Inquire at Bishop Marty's residence.

While his transfer to St. Cloud may have been planned by

others to reduce Bishop Marty's work load and mental burdens, he himself did not necessarily get the message. He established eight new parishes—at Browerville, Eden Valley, Mora, Browns Valley, Little Falls, Mayhew Lake, Flensburg and Moran. He laid the cornerstone for new churches in Wadena, Foley and Princeton, and in St. Cloud he planned the construction of an addition to the cathedral parish school while generally pursuing the other duties of his office. On April 17 he assisted as co-consecrator of Bishop Thomas O'Gorman, his successor in Sioux Falls, and on June 7 he delivered the funeral oration for Bishop Rupert Seidenbusch, who like himself had been a Benedictine monk and abbot.

Before he left the South Dakota diocese, he had insisted that he should be permitted to oversee the Sioux Indian missions as he had done in the past, and Bishop O'Gorman, a former professor at the Catholic University of America with no missionary experience, agreed to the arrangement. Consequently, Marty continued to make periodic trips to the reservations, especially to attend the annual Catholic Indian Congresses which he had first established in 1891.

The congresses were really an outgrowth of the Ghost Dance episode and the Wounded Knee debacle. Bishop Marty recognized well the Indians' nomadic spirit and their love of the traditional tribal reunions. He concluded that if the powwows could be replaced with a Christian festival each year, the meshing of the two cultures could be speeded.

National and religious holidays were festive occasions at the Fort Yates government school. Even after Bishop Marty was transferred to St. Cloud, Minnesota, he maintained a continuing interest in the educational work among the Sioux in the neighboring Dakotas. (Sacred Heart Convent archives)

The first congress took place at Standing Rock Agency during the week of the Fourth of July (which also permitted inclusion of American patriotic symbolism along with the religious theme). From throughout the Dakotas the Sioux traveled in the old way to a new festivity, erecting their tepees to form a giant encampment reminiscent of the past days of unfettered glory. Traditional orations of the chiefs, prowess competitions and extensive feasting were preserved as part of the program, but even more dominant were the rites and ecclesiastical pageantry of the Church.

Priests and catechists were busy with classes. From dawn to dusk the prairie confessionals served long lines of penitents. Such serious issues as the evils of divorce, drunkenness and sloth were discussed in council. The sacraments of baptism, confirmation and marriage were administered, and the four-day event was concluded with a solemn procession of the Blessed Sacrament led by mounted Sioux bearing the Cross of Christ and the American flag. Bishop Marty carried the monstrance under a canopy borne by uniformed Indian policemen, as white-clad girls scattered prairie flowers ahead of him.

The bishop's attendance at the festive congresses was a special treat, both for him and for the participants. He officiated formally at Mass and other ceremonious rituals which appealed to the Indians; and informally he shook their hands at the opening reception, visited with them and toured the camps as their honored guest. But even in this happy role he was not permitted respite from the controversy which plagued him so much during his final years.

Countering the Catholic congresses, the Episcopalians and Congregationalists held similar convocations and conferences in the fall, all of which caused Agent James McLaughlin to react to the practice. He was concerned because entire families took from two to six weeks to travel to and from the meetings, and in his official report he wrote:

> "These annual journeys, in large cavalcades, are looked forward to by the Indians for months in advance, in consequence of which many neglect cultivation of their fields and other necessary work, and to a majority of those participating, it simply takes the place of the annual hunt and summer encampment of the old Indian life."

As a result, McLaughlin recommended that the Catholic congresses and Protestant assemblies be attended by smaller groups of delegates, thus reducing the overall effect of the gatherings. He questioned that the Christian values gained overcame the economic loss. For a time, however, the yearly events continued, and it is very likely that Bishop Marty looked forward to them with as much anticipation and enthusiasm as the Indians themselves.

In the early summer of 1896 his health had deteriorated to such a degree that he was urged to pass up the sixth congress scheduled that year at Holy Rosary Mission on the Pine Ridge Reservation. The bishop disagreed, of course, and when the time came, he made the long rail and wagon trip through the oppressive mid-summer heat.

It was obvious to all when he arrived at the agency that the Black Robe Lean Chief had paid the price for his intense commitment. When he administered the sacrament of confirmation, he was so weak that he required the assistance of a younger priest to support him. Still, with a remarkable reserve of strength, he delivered a departing sermon (using an interpreter, even after 20 years, to make sure he was understood). He explained that in the future the congresses would be smaller, local affairs so that agricultural pursuits would not suffer; but more important, he urged all of his beloved Indian friends to remain true to the teachings he and his fellow missionaries had imparted to them.

And then the Siouian odyssey of the Swiss monk was ended!

From Pine Ridge he proceeded to St. Martin's Convent in Sturgis to conduct the annual retreat for the Benedictine sisters there. Earlier in the year he had made a similar visitation to Sacred Heart Convent in Yankton, a nostalgic homecoming to the mount which would henceforth bear his name. From the Black Hills he returned to St. Cloud, weakened but gratified—not yet ready to quit.

✠ ✠ ✠

On September 15 Bishop Marty was scheduled to dedicate St. Wendelin's Church at Luxemburg, Minnesota. He rose from a sick bed to make the wagon trip to the Stearns County community where he blessed the assembled parishioners on the eve of the ceremony. He was unable to eat any supper that night, and severe coughing spells kept him from restful sleep. Yet, he refused to take his medicine after midnight because he insisted upon maintaining the Eucharistic fast so he could say Mass the following morning. Somehow he managed to complete the Holy Sacrifice (his last), after which he was persuaded to forego the strenuous consecration ceremony and return to bed. That evening—feeling much better—he dictated 22 letters.

On the 16th he was again too ill to say Mass, but while the service was progressing, he got up from bed, dressed and walked to the church. In the sacristy he vested in cope and miter, took his crosier and entered the sanctuary during the last gospel. It was a tense, dramatic moment. From his throne at the high altar, he intoned the prescribed prayers of confirmation and then anointed the 70 young people who had been prepared for the sacrament. Two priests knelt on either side of him to support his arms, and twice he stopped to rest. With almost superhuman effort he sang the closing responses and then—in his final sermon—he emphasized again his fervent love for the Blessed Mother of God, a dominant theme of his entire religious life.

After leaving the church he suffered a fainting spell, but by mid-afternoon he felt strong enough to give orders to hitch up so he could return to the city. Bundled in a thick robe, he traveled the last of the long weary miles which, in his 62nd year, literally had worn him out. Two days later, on Saturday morning, September 19, 1896, he died in his episcopal residence at St. Cloud.

✠ ✠ ✠

In the black-and-white festooned Cathedral of St. Cloud, Bishop James McGolrick of Duluth was celebrant of the Solemn Requiem Mass. The funeral oration was delivered by Archbishop John Ireland of St. Paul, who in eloquent terms recounted the life's work of the self-sacrificing Swiss monk of monumental dedication:

> "We feel today that a Saint has passed from earth ... Bishop Marty did not live for himself. He lived for God and [his] neighbor ... Nothing did he seek for mere pleasure. He sought all things in the name of duty. His life was ... a life of poverty, giving nothing to himself except the bare necessaries ... Never did he utter one word of regret, and indeed it is well known that the illness from which he died ... arose from his privations as a missionary in the early days of Dakota ...
>
> "There was in him a passionate love for the American Indian ... The more destitute the poor savage, the more ardent Bishop Marty's zeal was for him ... He was always ready to devote himself to the savage and the civilized, to the poor and the rich, the ignorant and the learned. There was no distinction among men, and he had in this fulfilled the mission of a soul which lifts itself above all considerations of color and condition and nationality ...
>
> "Each man has some peculiar trait of character by which he is marked among his fellows. Bishop Marty's ... was his inflexible

obedience to his conscience . . . Whenever his conscience bade him act, nothing held him back. When his conscience told him to stop, all the powers of earth would not move him. His whole purpose in life was to harken to his conscience and to obey it, for he knew the voice of conscience was the voice of God . . ."

When the service in the overflowing cathedral had ended, the procession to the Calvary Hill cemetery began. Ahead of the horse-drawn hearse marched members of the Catholic Order of Foresters, St. Joseph Society, the Polish Club and the Catholic Teachers' Society of Stearns County. Sadly missing were any organized delegations of Sioux Indians who on so many other occasions had accompanied the bishop in colorful ceremony on the reservations. At the graveside Abbot Conrad Frowin of Conception Abbey led the commitment prayers for his lifelong friend and fellow Benedictine.

For Martin Marty, O.S.B., his *ora et labora* had been fulfilled.

An Epilogue

Cross, Crosier and Calumet

". . . hasten to do now what may profit us for eternity."
—Prologue to the Rule of St. Benedict

Like so many pioneers in different places and callings, Bishop Marty left a mixed legacy. Motivated and directed by the prevailing attitudes of his day, he devoted a large measure of his life to the Sioux Indians, serving them and instructing them in the ways he felt best. There was little effort at the time by *any* of the frontier missionaries to understand or relate the Indians' *Wakantanka* (the Great Spirit) to the Christian God. Consequently, some later-day critics have tended to belittle or even denigrate the labors of the reservation evangelists regardless of sect.

But Martin Marty was little concerned about historical analysis or posthumous recognition. He was merely following the will of God as it was revealed to him—and his only critic of consequence was his own conscience.

Though he wrote voluminously throughout his lifetime, the products of his pen were widely scattered or destroyed. Much of his correspondence related to practical matters: concern for the welfare of the Sioux, recruitment of priests and sisters, diocesan business and a broad spectrum of activities which burdened his mind.

Of his personal papers, very little remains. An overzealous housekeeper in St. Cloud apparently discarded much of his memorabilia. There is also evidence that Bishop O'Gorman, who succeeded Marty in Sioux Falls, was interrupted by a priest of the diocese as O'Gorman was methodically sorting his predecessor's letters and other documents and destroying most of them in a blazing fireplace. Despite the fact that he was recognized as an historian of some stature, the bishop seemingly made precipitous judgments regarding Marty's papers—especially those relating to personnel problems—and did away with them on the basis that it would be better for all concerned to "let sleeping dogs lie."

As is often the case with controversy, Bishop Marty's relationship with problem priests tends to be over-blown in retrospect when, in fact, the vast majority of clerics with whom he worked were, like himself, dedicated and devout. However, the difficulties which he *did* experience weighed so heavily upon him that his life was critically affected and most likely shortened as a result. Not all the priests who gave him troubles were rebels or misfits; some were simply irrepressible doers in his own mold—men who accepted frontier challenges and pushed ahead with little regard for precedent or permission.

Father Francis M. Craft, part Mohawk Indian with a medical education, was typical of those who—by their own imaginative and energetic actions—created unintentional aggravations for their bishop. Marty had high regard for Father Craft, a convert to Catholicism, who was assigned to the Rosebud Reservation after

Father William Kroeger, the pastor-physician of Epiphany, was not a "problem priest" for Bishop Marty, but his unusual dual role brought concerns about canonical conflict of interest. (Sacred Heart Convent archives)

the "peace policy" was revoked. There the exuberant priest sided with the Indians against the government agent and Protestant missionaries on the issue of sending tribal children away to school in Pennsylvania. Father Craft was ordered off the reservation, but Bishop Marty interceded to win a reversal of the edict. In the interests of harmony, however, he then transferred the indefatigable priest to the Fort Berthold Reservation in North Dakota where Father Craft continued what proved to be an unsuccessful attempt to establish an all-Indian sisterhood.

At the village of Epiphany in South Dakota, Bishop Marty had another unusual priestly representative. Father William Kroeger had received a diploma from the Ohio Medical School in Cincinnati before entering the seminary at St. Meinrad. In 1893 he came to the diocese of Sioux Falls in search of a better climate for his own health; and when the bishop assigned the priest-physician to the Hanson County parish, he suggested that the new pastor might give attention both to the bodies and souls of his parishioners. Before long Father Kroeger became widely known more as a doctor than as a priest, and patients came long distances to see him for a whole litany of ailments. In addition, he sent his

Vestiges of Bishop Marty's missionary service still exist at various locations within his old vicariate. This statue of the "Black Robe Lean Chief" memorializes him at St. Paul's Indian Mission, Marty, South Dakota. (Sacred Heart Convent archives)

-PEACE-

To Whom it may Concern:

This is to certify, that the enclosed souvenirs:
A linnen shirt, purple cloth, drinking cup, from which the Rt.Rev.Bishop Martin Marty, O.S.B. drank water a few moments before his holy death, pepper & salt shaker, towel, mirror, a lock of hair, were taken, with the kind consent of the Most Reverend Archbishop Ireland, of Saint Paul, Minn., from the saintly Bishop Marty, on the 19th day of Sept.1896.
Until the 19.of June, 1918, these relics were in possession of Miss Mary Goeden, for some time assistant Maid in the Bishop's House at Sioux Falls, S.D., and St.Cloud, Minn. On the 19.of June, 1918, these relics were given to Rev.Father Ignatius Forster, O.S.B., to be retained at Sacred Heart Convent, Yankton, S.D., where the Rt.Rev.Bishop resided for about 10 years. May the holy Bishop remember us at the throne of the Most High!
In witness thereof I have signed this with my own hand this. 7. day of July, 1918.

Mary Goeden

Sioux City, Iowa.

Signed Ignatius Forster O.S.B.
Witnesses: S. M. Thecla. O.S.B.

In his effort to preserve the memory of Bishop Marty, Father Ignatius Forster, O.S.B., documented what personal effects could be collected following the pioneer missionary's death. Most of the bishop's correspondence was destroyed, along with other papers relating to his Dakota service. The archives of Sacred Heart Convent, St. Meinrad Archabbey and Maria Einsiedeln contain limited memorabilia of his life. (Sacred Heart Convent archives) bottled medicines all over the country. There was some question regarding the propriety (if not canonical legality) of Father Kroeger's dual calling. However, Bishop Marty did not prohibit the unique arrangement, although it undoubtedly caused him some moments of concern. (Later, under Bishop O'Gorman, Father Kroeger discontinued his priestly ministry for a time to concentrate on his medical activities.)

Earlier, at Minot in northern Dakota, Marty had appointed Father F. J. McCabe as first resident pastor. A highly educated doctor of theology, the young priest had volunteered for service on the frontier. After only one month in the boisterous village, he sent a letter of resignation to Yankton. Father Vincent Wehrle recalled that when Father McCabe left the rugged Territory for more sophisticated regions, Bishop Marty merely commented, with obvious relief: "Thanks be to God that he is gone."

There were other priests, too, who—because of their special talents—functioned best with looser rein: like Father Peter Rosen, the geologist-historian in the Black Hills; the ambitious and autocratic Father Otto Zardetti, Marty's own vicar general; and even Father Chrysostom Foffa, the capable and resourceful Benedictine who shared some of Marty's earliest experiences on the plains. The bishop was well aware of the differences in personalities and abilities of individual priests and sisters, but though he made allowances in certain cases, personnel difficulties continued to plague him throughout much of his later career.

Bishop Marty himself was a man whose life generated what one author has referred to as "holy legends." Because he fearlessly and doggedly pursued his missionary calling among the Sioux, he achieved a notoriety during his lifetime which he never sought. His conferences with Sitting Bull, for instance, were particularly newsworthy at the time they occurred and then acquired fictionalized embellishments as the years passed.

Incidents of a miraculous nature were also attributed to the bishop, although documentation is flimsy. Soon after his arrival in Dakota Territory, he supposedly visited a Sioux camp where smallpox raged. After he had blessed the frightened people with his pectoral cross, it was reported that no new cases of the dread disease appeared.

At Holy Rosary Mission during the Messiah Craze, he was credited with restoring to normalcy a young Indian boy who, the sisters believed, was "possessed by the devil." And, some time after his death, when a violent storm threatened to destroy the church at St. Francis on the Rosebud Reservation, one of the sisters frantically rang the steeple bell which Marty had blessed. The other nuns prayed for the late bishop's intercession, and almost immediately the storm was said to have lost its fury.

Whether he had the power of miracles or not, Martin Marty was—as Father Albert Kuhn described him—"a man of no ordinary stamp." Like St. Benedict at Subiaco, he went forth among the pagans to spread the word of God. Also like St. Benedict, he gave the full measure of his physical being, participating as each did in final liturgical rites with their weary arms supported by others.

At St. Cloud, Minnesota, Bishop Marty's grave is marked by a simple granite monument; but at Yankton, South Dakota, the ma-

The Bishop Marty Memorial Chapel in Yankton was consecrated on April 18, 1950. Appropriately, the inside of the upper chapel was constructed of sandstone quarried at St. Meinrad, Indiana. Bishop William O. Brady, a successor to Marty in the diocese of Sioux Falls, officiated at the ceremony. Bede Hall, administration building of Mount Marty College, is adjacent to the chapel. (Sacred Heart Convent archives)

jestic spire of the Bishop Marty Memorial Chapel rises above the historic city on the western heights bearing his name. Mount Marty College, a four-year coeducational institution—established first as a junior college for women in 1936—grows in reputation on the same campus where the bishop once taught young Indian boys the Gregorian "plain song" and the rudiments of civilization. The adjoining Sacred Heart Hospital, founded by the Benedictine sisters he brought to the old territorial capital, officially does business as the Marty Hospital Association, Inc.

Elsewhere, in Charles Mix County, South Dakota, the tiny town of Marty recalls the pioneer missionary's visitations to the old Yankton Indian Reservation. Blue Cloud Abbey at Marvin, South Dakota, and Assumption Abbey at Richardton, North Dakota, stand as the belated fulfillment of Martin Marty's dream that Benedictine monasteries should rise above the plains to perpetuate the Rule and the tradition of *ora et labora* he brought to the region.

Though frustration and discouragement were with him almost constantly, adding mental burdens to his physical suffering, he complained little, he prayed much and he never faltered in his unstinting dedication to the work that "nobody else wanted to do."

Author's Acknowledgments

There is no more difficult part of a book to write than the Acknowledgments section. Not that the expression of appreciation is burdensome, but help usually comes from so many directions and from so many people that it weighs heavily upon an author to remember everyone who has contributed to the project in one way or another.

While I have collected material about Bishop Marty spasmodically for a good many years and knew the highlights of his story, I could never have written this book in the brief time allotted had it not been for the prior work of certain key people.

Most important was Father Ildefons Betschart of Einsiedeln, who completed an earlier biography of Marty in the centennial year of the latter's birth. Because I do not read German well, that book would have been of little value to me had it not been translated into English by Sister M. Stanislaus Van Well, who also provided a detailed editorial review of my manuscript.

Father Albert Kleber in his *History of St. Meinrad Archabbey, 1854-1954* chronicled an important phase in the monastic life of Martin Marty, while Sister M. Claudia Duratschek traced the bishop's involvement with the Benedictine Sisters of Sacred Heart Convent and kept me on solid historical ground with her well-researched books on the Catholic heritage in the Dakotas.

Sister Wilma Lyle, prioress of the Yankton religious community in its centennial year, provided the impetus, encouragement and editorial guidance which made the final product a reality. Board members of the Benedictine Service Fund were generously supportive of the endeavor.

As I worked on the manuscript, dozens of sisters stopped me in hallways, on street corners and in library reference rooms to ask how I was coming "on Bishop Marty." Their interest spurred me, of course; and one in particular—Sister Desideria Hirsch—was not only a constant source of information but her prayers in behalf of my labors undoubtedly gave me a dimension of assistance I needed more than any other.

Sister Jerome Schmitt offered me the advantage of special counsel; Sister Verena Kaiser in the convent archives and Sisters Elise Haverkamp and Grace Feldhacker in the library were cooperative and helpful. I am grateful also to Sisters Laurina Kaiser, Marie Helene Werdel, Jane and Jeanette Klimisch, Denise Stevens, Inez Welchert and other members of Sacred Heart Convent who assisted in numerous ways.

As she has done on so many other occasions, my wife, Phyllis, survived my bearishness during the writing period and by various wiles kept me at the typewriter until the job was done.

In the research department, special thanks must go to Glenn Sundvold and the Mount Marty College library; Les Helgeland and Ellen Tobin of the *Yankton Daily Press & Dakotan;* Dayton W. Canaday, Bonnie Gardner and Rosemary Evetts of the South Dakota Historical Resource Center, Pierre; and Donald J. Binder of the Yankton County Historical Society and Museum.

Among others who contributed to the project in one way or another were Fathers Thomas J. Ryan, Gary Ternes, Stanislaus Maudlin and Al Krzyzopolski; Monsignor Louis J. Delahoyde; Rose Ann Kawalczyk, county clerk of courts office, St. Cloud, Minnesota; Jeff Gunderson, Indiana Historical Society; Robert Frei, Verkehrsverein Einsiedeln, Switzerland; Pierre-Yves Simonin, cultural counselor for the Embassy of Switzerland, Washington, D. C.; Marguerite and Mrs. Robert Janousek; Marjorie Deist; Ronald D. Morton; and Dr. Willis F. Stanage. Glenn Gering of the Pine Hill Printery in Freeman, South Dakota, helped make the printing production process enjoyable rather than burdensome.

If, after all that, I have overlooked anyone, I can assure you that it was inadvertent and my thanks are herewith expressed apologetically to such forgotten benefactors in anonymity.

R.F.K.

Bibliography

Ahern, Rev. Patrick H., editor. *Catholic Heritage in Minnesota, North Dakota, South Dakota.* St. Paul, Minnesota: H. M. Smyth Co., 1964.

Assenmacher, Father Hugh, O.S.B. *A Place Called Subiaco.* Little Rock, Arkansas: Rose Publishing Co., 1977.

Bailey, Dana R. *History of Minnehaha County.* Sioux Falls, South Dakota: Brown and Saenger, 1899.

Barry, Father Colman J. *Worship and Work.* Collegeville, Minnesota: Saint John's Abbey, 1956.

Betschart, Father Ildefons, O.S.B. *Bishop Martin Marty, O.S.B., Apostle of the Sioux, 1834-1896.* Einsiedeln, Switzerland: Benziger & Co., 1934. (Translated from the German by Sister M. Stanislaus Van Well, O.S.B.)

Burton, Katherine. *The Golden Door: The Life of Katharine Drexel.* New York: P. J. Kennedy & Sons, 1957.

Casper, Father Henry W., S.J. *History of the Catholic Church in Nebraska* (Vol. II). Milwaukee, Wisconsin: The Bruce Publishing Company, 1966.

Dehey, Elinor Tong. *Religious Orders of Women in the United States.* Hammond, Indiana: W. B. Conkey Co., 1930.

Dudine, Sister M. Frederica, O.S.B. *The Castle on the Hill.* Milwaukee, Wisconsin: The Bruce Publishing Company, 1967.

Duratschek, Sister M. Claudia. *The Beginnings of Catholicism in South Dakota.* Washington, D. C.: The Catholic University Press, 1943.

——. *Crusading Along Sioux Trails.* St. Meinrad, Indiana: The Grail Press, 1947.

——. *Travelers on the Way of Peace.* Sioux Falls, South Dakota: Brown and Saenger, 1955.

——. *Under the Shadow of His Wings.* Aberdeen, South Dakota: North Plains Press, 1971.

Fitzgerald, Sister Mary Clement, P.B.V.M. "Bishop Marty and His Sioux

Missions, 1876-1896." *South Dakota Historical Collections* (Vol. XX). Pierre, South Dakota: State Historical Society, 1940.

Forster, Father Ignatius, O.S.B. "Bishop Martin Marty, O.S.B.—Apostle of the Sioux." *The Indian Sentinel,* Vol. 2, No. 1. Washington, D. C.: Bureau of Catholic Indian Missions, January, 1920.

Jäger, Father Moritz, O.S.B. *Sister Gertrude Leupi, 1825-1904.* Fribourg, Switzerland: Kanisius Verlag, 1974. (Translated from the German by Father Alexander J. Luetkemeyer, O.S.B.)

Janssen, Hans. "Bishop Martin Marty in the Dakotas." *The American-German Review,* June-July, 1961.

Karolevitz, Robert F. *Challenge: The South Dakota Story.* Sioux Falls, South Dakota: Brevet Press, Inc., 1975.

——. *Pioneer Church in a Pioneer City.* Aberdeen, South Dakota: North Plains Press, 1971.

——. *Yankton: A Pioneer Past.* Aberdeen, South Dakota: North Plains Press, 1972.

Kingsbury, George W. *History of Dakota Territory.* Chicago: S. J. Clarke Publishing Co., 1915.

Kleber, Father Albert, O.S.B. *History of St. Meinrad Archabbey, 1854-1954.* St. Meinrad, Indiana: The Grail Press, 1954.

Larkin, Georgia. *Chief Blue Cloud.* Marvin, South Dakota: Blue Cloud Abbey, 1964.

Locken, Sister M. Hermina, O.S.B. "The Most Reverend Martin Marty, O.S.B., First Bishop of Dakota and Apostle of the Sioux." Unpublished undergraduate thesis. Yankton, South Dakota: Mount Marty College, 1938.

Malone, Father Edward E., O.S.B. *A History of Conception Colony, Abbey and Schools.* Omaha, Nebraska: Interstate Printing Company, 1971.

Marty, Bishop Martin, O.S.B. *Dr. Johann Martin Henni, First Bishop and Archbishop of Milwaukee.* New York: Benziger Brothers, 1888.

McDonald, Sister M. Grace, O.S.B. *With Lamps Burning.* Saint Joseph, Minnesota: Saint Benedict's Priory Press, 1957.

Moynihan, James H. *The Life of Archbishop John Ireland.* New York: Harper & Brothers, 1953.

Pfaller, Father Louis L., O.S.B. *The Catholic Church in Western North Dakota, 1738-1960.* Mandan, North Dakota: Diocese of Bismarck, 1960.

——. *James McLaughlin: The Man with an Indian Heart.* New York: Vantage Press, 1978.

Rasmussen, Douglas James. *A Time to Be Born: The First Catholic Church in Dakota.* Vermillion, South Dakota: A Pax Book Bar Publication, 1975.

Reardon, James Michael, P.A. *The Catholic Church in the Diocese of St. Paul*. St. Paul, Minnesota: North Central Publishing Company, 1952.

Robinson, Doane. *History of South Dakota* (Vol I). Indianapolis, Indiana: B. F. Bowen & Co., 1904.

Robinson, Elwyn B. *History of North Dakota*. Lincoln, Nebraska: University of Nebraska Press, 1966.

Schell, Herbert S. *History of South Dakota*. Lincoln, Nebraska: University of Nebraska Press, 1961.

Van Zellen, Dom Hubert. *The Holy Rule*. New York: Sheed and Ward, 1958.

Vestal, Stanley. *Sitting Bull, Champion of the Sioux*. Boston: Houghton Mifflin Company, 1932.

In addition to the references above, the author utilized microfilms and files of various newspapers, principally the *Yankton Press and Dakotaian (Dakotan)* and the *Sioux Falls Press*. Also of particular value were the personal letters of Sister M. Mathilda Cattani, O.S.B., from the archives of Sacred Heart Convent; the limited available correspondence of Bishop Martin Marty himself; copies of *The Indian Sentinel*, published by the Bureau of Catholic Indian Missions; and the annual reports of the Commissioner of Indian Affairs to the Secretary of the Interior.

The Marty Council of the Knights of Columbus in Yankton erected a statue to the memory of its namesake bishop in 1919. First erected at the entry of Sacred Heart Convent as shown, the replica was later moved to a place of prominence in front of Bede Hall, Mount Marty College. (Sacred Heart Convent archives)

About the Author

Robert F. Karolevitz was born in Sacred Heart Hospital at Yankton, South Dakota, just a short distance from the historic residence of Bishop Martin Marty. He received his primary education from the Benedictine Sisters of Sacred Heart Convent and therefore developed an early interest in the story of the pioneer missionary.

After almost two decades on the West Coast, Karolevitz and his wife, Phyllis, re-established residence in their native state which has honored him as a charter inductee into the South Dakota Heritage Hall of Fame.

The Marty biography is his seventeenth book, several of which have won national and regional recognition. Most notable is *Where Your Heart Is,* the story of the Dakota-born artist, Harvey Dunn, which won for Karolevitz a coveted Wrangler statuette from the National Cowboy and Western Heritage Hall of Fame, Oklahoma City. *Pioneer Church in a Pioneer City,* an earlier book about Bishop Marty's procathedral in Yankton, was awarded a national certificate of commendation by the American Association of State and Local History.

Karolevitz is a graduate of South Dakota State University with a major in Printing and Rural Journalism. He has served as president of the University's Alumni Association and has received its Distinguished Alumni Award. He also holds a master's degree in journalism from the University of Oregon.

A veteran of World War II and the Korean conflict, he has been a newspaperman, ghost writer, military public information officer, advertising copywriter and public relations counsel. He is a life member of Sigma Delta Chi, professional journalistic society; was president of the Seattle, Washington, Advertising Club; and has served the South Dakota State Historical Society as a member of its executive board.

A small room in the Bishop Marty Memorial Chapel contains mementoes of the pioneer Benedictine missionary: his throne, crozier, tabernacle, crucifix, missal, vestments and other items of memorabilia still in existence. (Sacred Heart Convent archives)

Index

(Because Bishop Marty's name appears throughout the book, no references are made to him in this index. North and South Dakota cities and towns are listed by state even though the date of mention was during the territorial period.)

A

B

C

I

J

K

L

M

N

O

P

R

S

T

U

V

W

Y

Z

Colophon

This book was lithographed in Freeman, South Dakota, by Pine Hill Press. Headlines were set in *Crown Bold* and the text matter in *Excelsior.* Midwestern Paper Company supplied the paper, *Hammermill Vellum Offset.* The book was bound by Midwest Editions of Minneapolis, Minnesota.